PATTERNS AND THEMES

A Basic English Reader

SECOND EDITION

PATTERNS AND THEMES

A Basic English Reader

SECOND EDITION

Judy R. Rogers

Glenn C. Rogers

Morehead State University, Kentucky

Wadsworth Publishing Company
A Division of Wadsworth, Inc.
Belmont, California

English Editor:	John Strohmeier
Production:	Del Mar Associates
Print Buyer:	Bill Ralph
Designer:	Donna Davis
Copy Editor:	Andrea Olshevsky
Photo Researcher:	Lindsay Kefauver
Compositor:	TypeLink, Inc.
Cover:	John Odam
Signing Representative:	Mark Francisco

ISBN 0-534-08832-5

Printed in the United States of America

4   5   6   7   8   9   10—92   91   90

Library of Congress Cataloging-in-Publication Data

Patterns and themes.

   1. College readers.   2. English language—Rhetoric.
I. Rogers, Judy R.   II. Rogers, Glenn C.
PE1417.P358   1988   808'.0427   87-23105
ISBN 0-534-08832-5 (pbk.)

For John and James
with the hope that borrowed hours can be repaid

THEMATIC
TABLE OF CONTENTS

RHETORICAL
TABLE OF CONTENTS

ILLUSTRATION

DEFINITION

COMPARISON/CONTRAST

PREFACE

Patterns and Themes is a collection of readings and writing assignments especially for students enrolled in basic or developmental writing courses. This edition of *Patterns and Themes* continues to provide brief readings selected to stimulate interest and reinforce frequently used writing patterns. As in the first edition, the content of the selections will appeal to college readers, but the readability level is comfortable for basic writing students. This edition contains seven new selections by professional writers and three new student essays, including a brief library paper.

Arrangement of the Text   The selections are grouped, first of all, by theme. For many students, especially those not ready to study rhetorical patterns, this arrangement provides a natural way to integrate material. To freshen the text for continuing users, there are two changes in themes from the first edition, but all remain broad. The themes are common to large groups of people from diverse backgrounds, and thus we have been able to represent varying points of view on the same topic. The selections in this edition maintain the variety of the first edition: short stories, popular journalism, student essays, and even short, narrative poems. They are variously entertaining, informative, and thought provoking.

In an alternate table of contents, we have indicated the common rhetorical tools used by the writers included in *Patterns and Themes*. Basic writers generally understand and move naturally toward common organizational patterns. Thus we have chosen a number of examples of narration and description, often of personal experiences. But we have also included selections that exhibit development by other frequently used rhetorical modes.

Aids to Reading and Writing   To increase students' enjoyment of the material and to speed the development of their reading and writing skills, we have included several learning aids. "Looking Forward" gives brief biographical information about the authors (when relevant) and points students toward main ideas and important writing strategies. "Help with Words" offers short definitions, often drawn from context. "A Second Look" sends students back to selections to consider points of meaning and to look again at writing techniques. Sometimes students are asked to consider ideas from two or more of the selections within a unit, thereby increasing their awareness of thematic unity and differing writing techniques.

In addition, "Ideas for Writing" gives writing assignments for paragraphs and, more often, short essays. In the early units, the emphasis is on description and narration. Later assignments—like later reading selections—increase in difficulty and introduce definition, comparison, process, simple persuasion, and reports using outside sources. Realizing that basic writers advance at different rates, we continue to suggest topics for description and narration throughout. Many of the assignments are structured to help students move through the writing process, especially the prewriting or planning stage. Instructors may easily substitute their own topics while still following the suggestions for prewriting.

Finally, this edition includes a new learning aid, "Making Connections," that will help develop students' critical thinking skills while suggesting the thematic links within a unit. The questions and suggestions in "Making Connections" call upon students to compare, contrast, define, evaluate, identify values, recognize stereotypes, identify key issues, and perform other basic critical thinking tasks. These suggestions could lead to class or small group discussion or to writing assignments.

Rationale of *Patterns and Themes* This text originally grew out of our discontent with basic writing courses that were given almost exclusively to drill and practice. The sentence-combining exercises, the grammar drills, the punctuation lessons, and the pages of workbook assignments are no doubt helpful. But, if unleavened by other material, they frequently become tedious to students and instructors alike. Reading, group discussion, and frequent writing add interest to basic composition and, as a result, help students build skills more rapidly.

In *Errors and Expectations*, Mina Shaughnessy argues for integrated instruction in writing and reading. Her ideas, and those of many others, have helped to shape both the original and the second editions of this text. We hope that the student who uses *Patterns and Themes* will become the student Shaughnessy describes: "a more careful writer and a more critical reader."

Acknowledgments We wish to thank the reviewers who offered their suggestions for improving this edition: Ann B. Dobie, University of Southwestern Louisiana; Paul D. Hauser, Kirkwood Community College; and Rita Phipps, North Seattle Community College. We are especially indebted to Sandra Meyer, the Pennsylvania State University, for her very practical advice based on her classroom experience with the text. We also appreciate the assistance of John Strohmeir, English Editor, the staff at Wadsworth, and Nancy Sjoberg of Del Mar Associates. Finally our thanks go to Caroline Hamilton, whose mastery of word processing deserves wide recognition.

PATTERNS AND THEMES

A Basic English Reader

SECOND EDITION

MEMORIES

SALVATION

Langston Hughes

LOOKING FORWARD

Langston Hughes—playwright, poet, fiction writer, expert in jazz and folklore—was one of the most influential figures in the history of black American literature. In "Salvation," a section of his autobiography, Hughes recalls an experience from his youth that left him sad and disappointed. As you read, remember that a piece of writing should introduce and develop a main idea or central point. Hughes's main idea is introduced early. Watch for its development.

HELP WITH WORDS

fold *(paragraph 1):* a pen for sheep; here, a church or its congregation

escorted *(paragraph 1):* accompanied or led

rhythmical *(paragraph 3):* with regular accents or beats

dire *(paragraph 3):* dreadful

work-gnarled *(paragraph 4):* twisted from hard work

rounder *(paragraph 6):* a drunkard

serenely *(paragraph 7):* peacefully

ecstatic *(paragraph 14):* greatly joyful, delighted

1   I was saved from sin when I was going on thirteen. But not really saved. It happened like this. There was a big revival at my Auntie Reed's church. Every night for weeks there had been much preaching, singing, praying, and shouting, and some very hardened sinners had been brought to Christ, and the membership of the church had grown by leaps and bounds. Then just before the revival ended, they held a special meeting for children, "to bring the young lambs to the fold." My aunt spoke of it for days ahead. That night I was escorted to the front row and placed on the mourners' bench with all the other young sinners, who had not yet been brought to Jesus.

2   My aunt told me that when you were saved you saw a light, and something happened to you inside! And Jesus came into your life! And God was with you from then on! She said you could see and hear and feel Jesus in your soul. I believed her. I had heard a great many old people say the same thing and it seemed to me they ought to know. So I sat there calmly in the hot crowded church, waiting for Jesus to come to me.

3   The preacher preached a wonderful rhythmical sermon, all moans and shouts and lonely cries and dire pictures of hell, and then he sang a song about the ninety and nine safe in the fold, but one little lamb was left in the cold. Then he said, "Won't you come? Won't you come to Jesus? Young lambs, won't you come?" And he held out his arms to all us young sinners there on the mourners' bench. And the little girls cried. And some of them jumped up and went to Jesus right away. But most of us just sat there.

4   A great many old people came and knelt around us and prayed, old women with jet-black faces and braided hair, old men with work-gnarled hands. And the church sang a song about the lower lights are burning, some poor sinners to be saved. And the whole building rocked with prayer and song.

5   Still I kept waiting to see Jesus.

6   Finally all the young people had gone to the altar and were saved, but one boy and me. He was a rounder's son named Westley. Westley and I were surrounded by sisters and deacons praying. It was very hot in the church, and getting late now. Finally Westley said to me in a whisper: "Goddamn! I'm tired o' sitting here. Let's get up and be saved." So he got up and was saved.

7   Then I was left all alone on the mourners' bench. My aunt came and knelt at my knees and cried, while prayers and songs swirled all around me in the little church. The whole congregation prayed for me alone, in a mighty wail of moans and voices. And I kept waiting serenely for Jesus, waiting, waiting—but he didn't come. I wanted to see him, but nothing happened to me. Nothing! I wanted something to happen to me, but nothing happened.

8   I heard the songs and the minister saying: "Why don't you come? My dear child, why don't you come to Jesus? Jesus is waiting for you. He wants you. Why don't you come? Sister Reed, what is this child's name?"

9   "Langston," my aunt sobbed.

10   "Langston, why don't you come? Why don't you come and be saved? Oh, Lamb of God! Why don't you come?"

11   Now it was really getting late. I began to be ashamed of myself, holding everything up so long. I began to wonder what God thought about Westley, who certainly hadn't seen Jesus either, but who was now sitting proudly on the platform, swinging his knickerbockered legs and grinning down at me, surrounded by deacons and old women on their knees praying. God had not struck Westley dead for taking his name in vain or for lying in the temple. So I decided that maybe to save further trouble, I'd better lie, too, and say that Jesus had come, and get up and be saved.

12   So I got up.

13   Suddenly the whole room broke into a sea of shouting, as they saw me rise. Waves of rejoicing swept the place. Women leaped into the air. My aunt threw her arms around me. The minister took me by the hand and led me to the platform.

14   When things quieted down, in a hushed silence, punctuated by a few ecstatic "Amens," all the new young lambs were blessed in the name of God. Then joyous singing filled the room.

15   That night, for the last time in my life but one—for I was a big boy twelve years old—I cried. I cried, in bed alone, and couldn't stop. I buried my head under the quilts, but my aunt heard me. She woke up and told my uncle I was crying because the Holy Ghost had come into my life, and because I had seen Jesus. But I was really crying because I couldn't bear to tell her that I had lied, that I had deceived everybody in the church, and I hadn't seen Jesus, and that now I didn't believe there was a Jesus any more, since he didn't come to help me.

A SECOND LOOK

1. Pick out some descriptive words in paragraphs 3 and 4 that help you to picture the scene in the church.

2. Hughes uses time order to organize his narrative. Transitional words at the beginnings of paragraphs emphasize this pattern. Locate these linking words at the beginnings of paragraphs 5, 6, and 7. Are other paragraphs linked together in this way?

3. Although writers usually avoid using one-sentence paragraphs except in reproducing speech, Hughes uses two (paragraphs 5 and 12). What does he achieve by doing this?

4. Why does young Hughes pretend to feel something that he has not really experienced?

5. Read the last paragraph again and state, in one sentence, why Hughes is crying.

IDEAS FOR WRITING

Describe for a group of classmates something that happened to you when you were younger that left you frustrated or disappointed. Make sure your readers understand first what you expected to happen and then what actually happened.

After you choose the incident, write down everything you can remember about it. Do not worry about the order of your ideas or the mechanics of your writing. Just get your thoughts on paper. Then read through what you have written and select the details that seem most interesting and important. Mark these details so that you can refer to them later.

Next, decide how you will begin telling about your experience. Write the opening. Then continue describing the experience, using the details you have marked, until you reach the end. Your closing may explain why the incident was important (reread Hughes's last paragraph).

Finally, reread your paper to see whether it says exactly what you want it to say. Make sure that the ideas are clear and that the details support the main idea.

THE WOMAN WARRIOR

Maxine Hong Kingston

LOOKING FORWARD

Maxine Hong Kingston, born in California to Chinese parents, has become one of the most important of the modern Chinese American writers. She is the author of several books as well as a teacher of creative writing. In her autobiography, *The Woman Warrior*, Kingston recalls how, in her girlhood, she was caught between two cultures—the old one of China, which she had never seen, and the new one of America, which her family had not completely joined. In this selection we see her growing rebellion against the harshly antifeminist attitudes of the emigrant Chinese.

HELP WITH WORDS

emigrant *(paragraph 5):* a person who has left one region or country to move into another

talking-story *(paragraph 11):* telling a story

outward tendency *(paragraph 18):* refers to the usual custom among Chinese girls of leaving their families and becoming part of their husbands' families

1   **M**y American life has been such a disappointment.

2   "I got straight A's, Mama."

3   "Let me tell you a true story about a girl who saved her village."

4   I could not figure out what was my village. And it was important that I do something big and fine, or else my parents would sell me when we made our way back to China. In China there were solutions for what to do with little girls who ate up food and threw tantrums. You can't eat straight A's.

5   When one of my parents or the emigrant villagers said, "Feeding girls is feeding cowbirds," I would thrash on the floor and scream so hard I couldn't talk. I couldn't stop.

6   "What's the matter with her?"

7   "I don't know. Bad, I guess. You know how girls are. 'There's no profit in raising girls. Better to raise geese than girls.'"

8   "I would hit her if she were mine. But then there's no use wasting all that discipline on a girl. 'When you raise girls, you're raising children for strangers.'"

9   "Stop that crying!" my mother would yell. "I'm going to hit you if you don't stop. Bad girl! Stop!" I'm going to remember never to hit or to scold my children for crying, I thought, because then they will only cry more.

10   "I'm not a bad girl," I would scream. "I'm not a bad girl. I'm not a bad girl." I might as well have said, "I'm not a girl."

11   "When you were little, all you had to say was 'I'm not a bad girl,' and you could make yourself cry," my mother says, talking-story about my childhood.

12   I minded that the emigrant villagers shook their heads at my sister and me. "One girl—and another girl," they said, and made our parents ashamed to take us out together. The good part about my brothers being born was that people stopped saying, "All girls," but I learned new grievances. "Did you roll an egg on my face like that when I was born?" "Did you have a full-month party for me?" "Did you turn on all the lights?" "Did you send my picture to Grandmother?" "Why not? Because I'm a girl? Is that why not?" "Why didn't you teach me English?" "You like having me beaten up at school, don't you?"

13   "She is very mean, isn't she?" the emigrant villagers would say.

14   "Come, children. Hurry. Hurry. Who wants to go out with

Great-Uncle?" On Saturday mornings my great-uncle, the ex-river pirate, did the shopping. "Get your coats, whoever's coming."

15 "I'm coming. I'm coming. Wait for me."

16 When he heard girls' voices, he turned on us and roared, "No girls!" and left my sisters and me hanging our coats back up, not looking at one another. The boys came back with candy and new toys. When they walked through Chinatown, the people must have said, "a boy—and another boy—and another boy!" At my great-uncle's funeral I secretly tested out feeling glad that he was dead—the six-foot bearish masculinity of him.

17 I went away to college—Berkeley in the sixties—and I studied, and I marched to change the world, but I did not turn into a boy. I would have liked to bring myself back as a boy for my parents to welcome with chickens and pigs. That was for my brother, who returned alive from Vietnam.

18 If I went to Vietnam, I would not come back; females desert families. It was said, "There is an outward tendency in females," which meant that I was getting straight A's for the good of my future husband's family, not my own. I did not plan ever to have a husband. I would show my mother and father and the nosey emigrant villagers that girls have no outward tendency. I stopped getting straight A's.

A SECOND LOOK

1. Why is Kingston's family not impressed that young Maxine got straight A's?

2. Explain what Kingston means in paragraph 10.

3. What kinds of distinctions does the family make between sons and daughters?

4. In what ways does Kingston rebel against the culture that rejected her? Why does she choose the strategy she does?

IDEAS FOR WRITING

Have you ever been in serious disagreement with the attitudes and beliefs of your family? Write about this situation, telling your readers (a group of people your own age) what these beliefs were and describing how you rebelled against them. Your essay should give clear answers to these questions:

1. What were the beliefs you and your family disagreed over?

2. How did you and the family express your feelings? Give examples.

3. Were you able to settle these differences? If so, how? If not, what have been the results of your continued disagreement?

DOWN THESE MEAN STREETS

Piri Thomas

LOOKING FORWARD

Piri Thomas was born to Puerto Rican parents in Spanish Harlem. In his twenties, Thomas, a drug user, was imprisoned for attempted armed robbery. Cured of his addiction and released from prison, he became a drug rehabilitation worker in Spanish Harlem and Puerto Rico. In an early chapter of his autobiography, *Down These Mean Streets*, Thomas writes about his hatred of school and teachers. In this selection he tells about one of his many conflicts in the classroom. Notice how this street-smart kid can turn a bad situation partly to his own advantage.

HELP WITH WORDS

muted *(paragraph 15):* quiet

Qué pasa? *(paragraph 17):* What's the matter? (Spanish)

chastised *(paragraph 20):* punished

intention *(paragraph 25):* wish, purpose

discretion *(paragraph 39):* caution

valor *(paragraph 39):* bravery

padre *(paragraph 41):* father (Spanish)

muchacho *(paragraph 43):* boy (Spanish)

1 One class I didn't dig at all was the so-called "Open Air Class" for skinny, "underweight" kids. We had to sleep a couple of half hours every day, and we got extra milk and jelly and peanut butter on brown bread. The teacher, Miss Shepard, was like a dried-up grape. One day I raised my hand to go to the toilet, but she paid me no mind. After a while, the pain was getting bad, so I called out, "Miss Shepard, may I leave the room?"

2 She looked up and just shook her head, no.

3 "But I gotta go, Miss Shepard."

4 "You just went a little while ago," she said.

5 "I know, Miss Shepard, but I gotta go again."

6 "I think it's sheer nonsense," said the old bitch. "You just want an excuse to play around in the hallways." . . .

7 I had to go so badly that I felt the tears forming in the corners of my eyes to match the drops that were already making a wet scene down my leg. "I'm goin' anyway," I said, and started toward the door.

8 Miss Shepard got up and screamed at me to get back to my seat. I ignored her.

9 "Get back to your seat, young man," she screamed. "Do you hear me? Get right back —" . . .

10 I reached the door and felt her hands grab out at me and her fingers hook on to the back of my shirt collar. My clean, washed-a-million-times shirt came apart in her hand.

11 I couldn't see her face clearly when I turned around. All I could think about was my torn shirt and how this left me with only two others. All I could see was her being the cause of the dampness of my pants and hot pee running down my leg. All I could hear was the kids making laughing sounds and the anger of my being ashamed. I didn't think of her as a woman, but as something that had to be hit. I hit it . . . .

12 "You struck me! You *struck* me! Oh, help, help!" she cried.

13 I cut out. Man, I ran like hell into the hallway, and she came right after me, yelling, "Help, help!" I was scared now and all I could think about was getting back to my Moms, my home, my block, where no one could hurt me. I ran toward the stairway and found it blocked off by a man, the principal. I cut back toward the back stairs.

14 "Stop him! Stop him!" dear Miss Shepard yelled, pointing her finger at me. "He struck me, he struck me."

15 I looked over my shoulder and saw the principal talk to her for

a hot second and then take off after me, yelling: "Stop! Stop!" I hit the stairs and went swooming down like it was all one big step. The principal was fast and I could hear him swearing right behind me. I slammed through the main-floor door that led to the lunchroom and jumped over benches and tables, trying like hell to make the principal trip and break a leg. Then I heard a muted cry of pain as a bench caught him in the shin. I looked over my shoulder and I dug his face. The look said that he was gonna hit me; that he wasn't gonna listen to my side of the story; that I had no side. I figured I better not get caught.

16   I busted my legs running toward the door that led to the outside and freedom, and with both hands out in front of me I hit the brass bar that opens the door. Behind me I heard a thump as the principal smacked into it. I ran down the block, sneaking a look behind me. The principal was right behind me, his face redder and meaner. People were looking at the uneven contest.

17   I tore into my hallway, screaming as loud as I could for help. The apartment doors opened up, one right after another. Heads of all colors popped out. "*Qué pasa?*" asked a Puerto Rican woman. "Wha's happenin'?" said a colored lady.

18   "They wanna beat me up in school and that's one of them," I puffed, pointing at the principal, who was just coming into view.

19   "Hooo, ain't nobody gonna hurt you, sonny," said the colored lady, whose name was Miss Washington. She gently pushed me behind her with one hand and with the other held it out toward the principal roaring down at us.

20   The principal, blocked by Miss Washington's 280 pounds and a look of "Don't you touch that boy," stopped short and puffed out, "That—that—kid—he—punched a teacher and—he's got to be chastised for it. After all, school disci—"

21   "Now hol' on, white man," Miss Washington interrupted. "There ain't nobody gonna chaz—whatever it is—this boy. I knows him an' he's a good boy—at least good for what comes outta this heah trashy neighborhood—an' you ain't gonna do nuttin' to him, unless you-all wan's to walk over me."

22   Miss Washington was talking real bad-like. I peeked out from behind that great behind.

23   "Madam, I assure you," the principal said, "I didn't mean harming him in a bodily manner. And if you knew the whole issue, you would agree with me that he deserves being chastised. As principal of his school, I have his best interest at heart. Ha, ha,

ha," he added, "you know the old saying, madam, 'A stitch in time saves nine.' Ha, ha, ha—*ahurmph.*"

24   I could see him putting that stitch in my head.

25   "I assure you, madam," he continued, smilingly pretty, "we have no intention of doing him bodily harm."

26   Once again I peeked out from behind Miss Washington's behind. "Yeah, that's what you say," I said. "How about alla time you take kids down to your office for some crap and ya start poking 'em with that big finger of yours until they can't take it any more?"

27   There were a lot of people in the hall by this time. They were all listening, and I knew it. "Yeah, ask any of the kids," I added. "They'll tell ya." I looked sorry-like at the crowd of people, who were now murmuring mean-like and looking at the principal like he didn't have long on this earth.

28   Smelling a Harlem lynch party in the making, I said, "An'—you—ain't—gonna—do—it—to—me. I'll get me a forty-five an'—"

29   "Hush you mouth, boy," Miss Washington said; "don't be talkin' like that. We grownups will get this all straightened out. An' nobody's gonna poke no finger in your chest"—she looked dead at the principal—"is they?"

30   The principal smiled the weakest smile in this smiling world. "I—I—I—er, assure you, madam, this young man is gifted with the most wonderful talent for prevarication I've ever seen."

31   "What's that mean?" Miss Washington asked suspiciously.

32   "Er, it means a good imagination, madam. A-ha-ha—yes, *ahurmph.*"

33   "That's a lie, Miss Washington," I said. "He's always telling the kids that. We asked Mrs. Wagner, the history teacher, and she said it means to lie. Like he means I'm a liar."

34   The look in the principal's eye said, "Oh, you smarty pants bastard," but he just smiled and said nothing.

35   Miss Washington said, "Iffen thar's any pokin' ta be done, we all heah is gonna do it," and she looked hard at the principal. The crowd looked hard at the principal. Hard sounds were taking forms, like, "So this is the way they treat our kids in school?" and "What you-all expect? These heah white people doan give a damn," and "If they evah treats mah boy like that, I'd . . . ."

36   The principal, smiling softly, began backing up.

37   I heard Momma's voice: "Piri, Piri, *qué pasa?*"

38 "Everything all right, Mis' Thomas," Miss Washington assured her. "This heah man was tryin' to hit your son, but ain't, 'cause I'll break his damn head wide open." Miss Washington shifted her weight forward. "Damn, Ah got a good mind to do it right now," she added.

39 The principal, remembering the bit about discretion being the better part of valor, split.

40 Everyone tried to calm Moms down. I felt like everybody there was my family. I let Momma lead me upstairs to our apartment. Everyone patted me on the head as we went by.

41 "You're going to school with your *padre* in the morning," Momma said.

42 "Uh-uh, Moms," I said. "That principal will stomp my chest in with that finger of his."

43 "No he won't, *muchacho*. Your father will go with you an' everything will be fixed up."

44 I just nodded my head and thought how great it would be if Miss Washington could go with me.

A SECOND LOOK

1. Thomas uses much direct quotation in his writing. How does he make the voices of Miss Shepard, the principal, and Miss Washington sound different?

2. How is the voice or style of the narrator (the adult Thomas) different from the voice of the student (young Piri)?

3. At the end of paragraph 11, Thomas says, "I hit it." Why does he use the pronoun *it* instead of *her*?

4. What does Thomas mean when he says he smells "a Harlem lynch party in the making" (paragraph 28)? Is he exaggerating?

5. Miss Washington and the principal take sides and act quickly in this situation because they act on the basis of group values that they have accepted. What are these values in each case?

IDEAS FOR WRITING

1. Tell about a situation in school or elsewhere in which you found yourself in trouble with those in authority. Begin by setting up the

circumstances and introducing the people you will write about. (Notice that Thomas describes Miss Shepard briefly. He doesn't describe the principal at first; we learn about the principal through what he says and does.) Then show how the situation developed, what actions took place, and how it ended.

2. Describe a teacher you liked or disliked very much. You will want to tell what the teacher looked like, how he or she behaved in class, and why you liked or disliked this person. You may use brief stories to help your readers understand what kind of person the teacher was.

3. Look at paragraphs 15 and 16 of Thomas's narrative. His description is alive and exciting because he uses many active, lively verbs. Try writing a paragraph in which you describe some brief but vigorous physical action—for example, running through a crowded place, lifting a heavy weight, passing a football, serving in tennis, chasing or being chased by an animal, and so on. Use as many lively and specific verbs as you can.

MY FIRST HUNTING TRIP

John Bennett

LOOKING FORWARD

This essay was written by a freshman composition student. As in Langston Hughes's "Salvation," the main idea here concerns the difference between what Bennett expected and what really happened. To make his point, he emphasizes how he feels at different times during the hunting trip.

HELP WITH WORDS

foraging *(paragraph 6):* searching for food

replica *(paragraph 6):* a copy

mauling *(paragraph 11):* injuring by rough treatment

---

1 It seems as if the cold is what I remember most.

2 The three of us (Tom, Dad, and I) rode in Tom's old pickup, sitting on our hands to keep them warm. I had been on hunting trips before, but this one was different. For the first time, I was allowed to carry a gun—an overused Winchester 20-gauge that was nearly as big as I was.

3   There was snow on the ground—three, maybe four inches. The drive to our old farm was painfully long, but we arrived just before dawn. We quickly unpacked, loaded our guns, and headed along an old road toward a dense group of briars, fallen trees, and young saplings. The two beagles we had brought along as "flushers" scurried from tree to bush, eagerly sniffing some day-old scent.

4   When we reached the top of the hill, two rabbits broke behind us. My dad and Tom shot once apiece, missing each time. I mumbled something about being too cold to move and walked on.

5   My task, I soon learned, was to sit and wait at the edge of the dense forest while Tom and Dad took the two dogs in. Supposedly, they would flush the rabbits out so I could get a shot. It sounded a bit suspicious to me, but I was tired from walking anyway.

6   I watched them disappear into the brush and sat down on a damp, rotten log. I then concentrated on observing the tree line I was stationed upon; no movement, not even the slightest change went unnoticed. After a while, large clumps of grass began to imitate foraging rabbits. Only a sudden gust of wind saved one extremely life-like replica, some forty-five yards away.

7   I laid my gun on one side of the log and put both of my hands inside my wool jacket in a fruitless attempt to keep them warm. It was no use; my fingers became numb and lifeless. There was no shelter from the wind, and every five minutes or so I would shake my arms like an injured bird, trying to create some body heat.

8   Up ahead, about seventy-five yards, the smaller of the two dogs came out of the foliage, ran toward me for twenty feet, and then was lost again in the brush. He was obviously on to something.

9   I suddenly became unaware of the cold as I reached for my gun. The same fingers that just before were blue and numb clicked the safety off. Trying to get a better look, I stood up above the weeds. I felt my heart quicken its pace, and I felt myself begin to tremble. Not from cold, however—I was no longer cold—but I trembled with an anticipation of what I somehow knew would come. I loosened the top button of my hunting vest and waited.

10   The rabbit appeared about fifty yards away, oblivious to my presence. I knew it was too far away for a certain kill shot, so I slowly knelt down and tried to hide. The rabbit, intent on escaping from the dog on its trail, came directly toward me until it was in range. I rose, ready for my prey to bolt away in fear. Instead,

the rabbit continued toward me, and then stopped five yards away from the gun barrel pointed at its head. It sat there, partially obscured by the snow, mocking the fact that I held its life in my right index finger.

11   I was confused, uncertain. This wasn't how it was supposed to be, not how I had seen it before. There was no sport (a favorite hunter's word) in mauling a rabbit sitting fifteen feet away. The rabbit wouldn't move, even when I stomped my foot in the snow.

12   I could not let my chance pass. Bracing myself for the recoil of my weapon, I squeezed the trigger and watched my prey fall into the blood-stained snow.

13   My trembling had stopped, and I realized that my bottom layer of clothes was soaked with perspiration. I sat down beside the rabbit, watching its back legs writhe violently.

14   "Reflexes," I told myself.

15   Tom and Dad approached me from behind. Seeing the rabbit, now still and cold in the snow, they congratulated me on my first kill. I watched Tom field dress the rabbit as he told me of his first rabbit.

16   I wasn't listening much. It had become cold again, and I turned my back to the wind.

A SECOND LOOK

1. Bennett emphasizes the cold, beginning with the first sentence. What details indicate how cold he feels? Why does he feel cold again after shooting the rabbit?

2. What other kinds of details does the author use in the first three paragraphs?

3. What does paragraph 6 indicate about the author's state of mind? (Note that he shows us rather than tells us.)

IDEAS FOR WRITING

1. Write a paragraph describing a time when you were unusually cold, hot, or wet, for instance. Concentrate on using sense words. To get

started, list as many words as you can think of that describe how you felt. Choose several of the most vivid ones to include in your paragraph.

2. Write about an important experience in your life that taught you something about yourself. Be sure that the main idea is clear, even if it is not stated in your essay.

MAKING CONNECTIONS

The essays of Langston Hughes, Maxine Kingston, and John Bennett all recall disillusioning experiences that left the young people with a feeling different from the one their cultures had led them to expect. Is the disillusionment necessary to their growing up? Does each young person learn some important reality?

FAMILIES

DISCOVERY OF A FATHER

Sherwood Anderson

LOOKING FORWARD

Sherwood Anderson, one of the major American novelists of this century, often drew upon the experiences of his own life for his writing. In this autobiographical essay, Anderson tells about a time in his childhood in the late 1800s. He describes his father mainly by telling how he behaved and how others reacted to him. As you read, decide what Anderson means by the word *discovery*.

HELP WITH WORDS

burr *(paragraph 11):* a Scots accent

orderly *(paragraph 21):* an enlisted man who aids an officer

immaculate *(paragraph 23):* perfectly clean, spotless

1   You hear it said that fathers want their sons to be what they feel they cannot themselves be, but I tell you it also works the other way. A boy wants something very special from his father. I know that as a small boy I wanted my father to be a certain thing he was not. I wanted him to be a proud, silent,

dignified father. When I was with other boys and he passed along the street, I wanted to feel a flow of pride: "There he is. That is my father."

2 But he wasn't such a one. He couldn't be. It seemed to me then that he was always showing off. Let's say someone in our town had got up a show. They were always doing it. The druggist would be in it, the shoe-store clerk, the horse doctor, and a lot of women and girls. My father would manage to get the chief comedy part. It was, let's say, a Civil War play and he was a comic Irish soldier. He had to do the most absurd things. They thought he was funny, but I didn't.

3 I thought he was terrible. I didn't see how mother could stand it. She even laughed with the others. Maybe I would have laughed if it hadn't been my father.

4 Or there was a parade, the Fourth of July or Decoration Day. He'd be in that, too, right at the front of it, as Grand Marshal or something, on a white horse hired from a livery stable.

5 He couldn't ride for shucks. He fell off the horse and everyone hooted with laughter, but he didn't care. He even seemed to like it. I remember once when he had done something ridiculous, and right out on Main Street, too. I was with some other boys and they were laughing and shouting at him and he was shouting back and having as good a time as they were. I ran down an alley back of some stores and there in the Presbyterian Church sheds I had a good long cry.

6 Or I would be in bed at night and father would come home a little lit up and bring some men with him. He was a man who was never alone. Before he went broke, running a harness shop, there were always a lot of men loafing in the shop. He went broke, of course, because he gave too much credit. He couldn't refuse it and I thought he was a fool. I had got to hating him.

7 There'd be men I didn't think would want to be fooling around with him. There might even be the superintendent of our schools and a quiet man who ran the hardware store. Once I remember there was a white-haired man who was a cashier of the bank. It was a wonder to me they'd want to be seen with such a windbag. That's what I thought he was. I know now what it was that attracted them. It was because life in our town, as in all small towns, was at times pretty dull and he livened it up. He made them laugh. He could tell stories. He'd even get them to singing.

8 If they didn't come to our house they'd go off, say at night, to

where there was a grassy place by a creek. They'd cook food there and drink beer and sit about listening to his stories.

9   He was always telling stories about himself. He'd say this or that wonderful thing had happened to him. It might be something that made him look like a fool. He didn't care.

10   If an Irishman came to our house, right away father would say he was Irish. He'd tell what county in Ireland he was born in. He'd tell things that happened there when he was a boy. He'd make it seem so real that, if I hadn't known he was born in southern Ohio, I'd have believed him myself.

11   If it was a Scotchman the same thing happened. He'd get a burr into his speech. Or he was a German or a Swede. He'd be anything the other man was. I think they all knew he was lying, but they seemed to like him just the same. As a boy that was what I couldn't understand.

12   And there was mother. How could she stand it? I wanted to ask but never did. She was not the kind you asked such questions.

13   I'd be upstairs in my bed, in my room above the porch, and father would be telling some of his tales. A lot of father's stories were about the Civil War. To hear him tell it he'd been in about every battle. He'd known Grant, Sherman, Sheridan and I don't know how many others. He'd been particularly intimate with General Grant so that when Grant went East, to take charge of all the armies, he took father along.

14   "I was an orderly at headquarters and Sim Grant said to me, 'Irve,' he said, 'I'm going to take you along with me.'"

15   It seems he and Grant used to slip off sometimes and have a quiet drink together. That's what my father said. He'd tell about the day Lee surrendered and how, when the great moment came, they couldn't find Grant.

16   "You know," my father said, "about General Grant's book, his memoirs. You've read of how he said he had a headache and how when he got word that Lee was ready to call it quits, he was suddenly and miraculously cured."

17   "Huh," said father. "He was in the woods with me."

18   "I was in there with my back against a tree. I was pretty well corned. I had got hold of a bottle of pretty good stuff.

19   "They were looking for Grant. He had got off his horse and come into the woods. He found me. He was covered with mud."

20   "I had the bottle in my hand. What'd I care? The war was over. I knew we had them licked."

21   My father said that he was the one who told Grant about Lee. An orderly riding by had told him, because the orderly knew how thick he was with Grant. Grant was embarrassed.

22   "But, Irve, look at me. I'm all covered with mud," he said to father.

23   And then, my father said, he and Grant decided to have a drink together. They took a couple of shots and then, because he didn't want Grant to show up potted before the immaculate Lee, he smashed the bottle against the tree.

24   "Sim Grant's dead now and I wouldn't want it to get out on him," my father said.

25   That's just one of the kind of things he'd tell. Of course the men knew he was lying, but they seemed to like it just the same.

26   When we got broke, down and out, do you think he ever brought anything home? Not he. If there wasn't anything to eat in the house, he'd go off visiting around at farmhouses. They all wanted him. Sometimes he'd stay away for weeks, mother working to keep us fed, and then home he'd come bringing, let's say, a ham. He'd got it from some farmer friend. He'd slap it on the table in the kitchen. "You bet I'm going to see that my kids have something to eat," he'd say, and mother would just stand smiling at him. She'd never say a word about all the weeks and months he'd been away, not leaving us a cent for food. Once I heard her speaking to a woman in our street. Maybe the woman had dared to sympathize with her. "Oh," she said, "it's all right. He isn't ever dull like most of the men in this street. Life is never dull when my man is about."

27   But often I was filled with bitterness, and sometimes I wished he wasn't my father. I'd even invent another man as my father. To protect my mother I'd make up stories of a secret marriage that for some strange reason never got known. As though some man, say the president of a railroad company or maybe a Congressman, had married my mother, thinking his wife was dead and then it turned out she wasn't.

28   So they had to hush it up but I got born just the same. I wasn't really the son of my father. Somewhere in the world there was a very dignified, quite wonderful man who was really my father. I even made myself half believe these fancies.

29   And then there came a certain night. He'd been off somewhere for two or three weeks. He found me alone in the house, reading by the kitchen table.

30   It had been raining and he was very wet. He sat and looked at me for a long time, not saying a word. I was startled, for there was on his face the saddest look I had ever seen. He sat for a time, his clothes dripping. Then he got up.

31   "Come on with me," he said.

32   I got up and went with him out of the house. I was filled with wonder but I wasn't afraid. We went along a dirt road that led down into a valley, about a mile out of town, where there was a pond. We walked in silence. The man who was always talking had stopped his talking.

33   I didn't know what was up and had the queer feeling that I was with a stranger. I don't know whether my father intended it so. I don't think he did.

34   The pond was quite large. It was still raining hard and there were flashes of lightning followed by thunder. We were on a grassy bank at the pond's edge when my father spoke, and in the darkness and rain his voice sounded strange.

35   "Take off your clothes," he said. Still filled with wonder, I began to undress. There was a flash of lightning and I saw that he was already naked.

36   Naked, we went into the pond. Taking my hand he pulled me in. It may be that I was too frightened, too full of a feeling of strangeness, to speak. Before that night my father had never seemed to pay any attention to me.

37   "And what is he up to now?" I kept asking myself. I did not swim very well, but he put my hand on his shoulder and struck out into the darkness.

38   He was a man with big shoulders, a powerful swimmer. In the darkness I could feel the movement of his muscles. We swam to the far edge of the pond and then back to where we had left our clothes. The rain continued and the wind blew. Sometimes my father swam on his back and when he did he took my hand in his large powerful one and moved it over so that it rested always on his shoulder. Sometimes there would be a flash of lightning and I could see his face quite clearly.

39   It was as it was earlier, in the kitchen, a face filled with sadness. There would be the momentary glimpse of his face and then again the darkness, the wind and the rain. In me there was a feeling I had never known before.

40   It was a feeling of closeness. It was something strange. It was as though there were only we two in the world. It was as though I

had been jerked suddenly out of myself, out of my world of the
schoolboy, out of a world in which I was ashamed of my father.

41   He had become blood of my blood; he the strong swimmer and I
the boy clinging to him in the darkness. We swam in silence and
in silence we dressed in our wet clothes, and went home.

42   There was a lamp lighted in the kitchen and when we came in,
the water dripping from us, there was my mother. She smiled at
us. I remember that she called us "boys."

43   "What have you boys been up to?" she asked, but my father did
not answer. As he had begun the evening's experience with me in
silence, so he ended it. He turned and looked at me. Then he went,
I thought, with a new and strange dignity out of the room.

44   I climbed the stairs to my own room, undressed in the darkness
and got into bed. I couldn't sleep and did not want to sleep. For the
first time I knew that I was the son of my father. He was a story
teller as I was to be. It may be that I even laughed a little softly
there in the darkness. If I did, I laughed knowing that I would
never again be wanting another father.

A SECOND LOOK

1. List several of his father's habits that embarrass Anderson. Why do
   they not embarrass his mother?

2. How do both the boy and the father change?

3. In what way does Anderson discover that he and his father are alike?

4. The language of this essay is often colloquial—that is, it has characteristics found more often in speech than in writing. Note the use of
   such phrases as "showing off," "got up a show," and "couldn't ride for
   shucks" (paragraphs 2 and 5). Can you find other examples? Also
   note that some sentences (or even paragraphs) are linked together
   with "and," "but," and "or." Find several examples. Anderson writes
   this way because he is trying to create the impression of telling a
   story aloud in the words of a person from a particular part of the
   country.

IDEAS FOR WRITING

1. In one or two paragraphs, give a detailed physical description of your
   mother, father, or other member of your family. Make a list of physi-

cal characteristics and then choose those that seem most important or special. Be specific. Do not use general statements such as "She is tall" or "He has dark hair." Instead, tell exactly how tall she is or exactly what color his hair is. Assume that you have asked a friend who has never met this relative to pick him or her up at the bus station while you are in class. Try to describe your subject so well that your friend might recognize this relative by reading your description.

2. Describe a family member or friend you feel very close to. Begin with a brief physical description. (See the writing suggestions in 1.) Then go on to explain what this person is like inside. Make notes on habits the person has, unusual attitudes he or she holds, or how the person gets along with others. Perhaps you can think of things this person has done that would help explain what he or she is like. Remember that you are writing for readers who do not know this person, and you want them to understand why he or she is special to you.

BECOMING HELPLESS

Colette Dowling

LOOKING FORWARD

This selection from Colette Dowling's book *The Cinderella Complex* explains some of the ways that women are taught dependence and submissiveness within their families at an early age. Dowling's father forcefully argued for her to accept his ideas and attitudes. Her mother was already dominated by the father's stronger personality. Dowling's self-examination leads her to believe that women are often actually afraid to succeed, a problem she calls the Cinderella complex.

HELP WITH WORDS

metronome *(paragraph 1):* an instrument for marking time

chronic *(paragraph 1):* long-lasting

elusiveness *(paragraph 2):* the quality of being hard to know or understand

confrontation *(paragraph 2):* a face-to-face conflict

intimidated *(paragraph 2):* made timid

palpable *(paragraph 2):* easily seen

loomed *(paragraph 3):* appeared

didactic *(paragraph 3):* inclined to teach or lecture others

authoritarian *(paragraph 3):* domineering

impinged *(paragraph 3):* crowded in on

lavishing *(paragraph 3):* giving freely

exuded *(paragraph 4):* sent out

disdain *(paragraph 7):* scorn or contempt

digress *(paragraph 7):* to wander from the topic

infusing *(paragraph 7):* pouring into

fledgling *(paragraph 8):* an inexperienced person

ruddy *(paragraph 8):* healthy red color

---

1   For many years I thought that my problems had to do with my father. Not until I was in my thirties did I begin to suspect that feelings about my mother were part of the inner conflict that had begun developing in me when I was very young. My mother was an even-tempered person, not given to screaming or fits of temper, always there, always waiting when my brother and I came home from school. She took me to dance lessons when I was very small, and later—until I was well into my teens—insisted that I practice the piano every day. She would sit by me and count, as regular and predictable as a metronome. Equally predictable was the afternoon nap she took, the small retreat from the reality of her daily life. She was given to illnesses of a chronic variety: headaches, bursitis, fatigue.

2   On the surface, there didn't seem to be anything so unusual about her life: she was the typical housewife/mother of her time. And yet . . . that peculiar elusiveness, and the little illnesses, so many of which, I think now (and so does she), were related to unexpressed anger. She avoided confrontation with my father and appeared to us children to be thoroughly intimidated by him. When she did speak out on some issue, the strain it caused her was palpable. She feared him.

3   In comparison with my mother, my father loomed large and vivid in my life—forceful Father with the big voice, big gestures, rude and sometimes embarrassing ways. He was didactic, authoritarian, and no one who knew him could easily dismiss him. Dislike, yes; there were certainly those who could summon forth that sentiment. But no one could pretend he wasn't there. He forced himself upon the consciousness of those with whom he came into contact; his personality impinged. You thought that he was lavishing attention upon you, but often the conversations seemed to spring more from some hidden need of his own.

4   I loved him. I adored the sureness he exuded, the idealism, the high, edgy energy. His laboratory in the engineering building at Johns Hopkins University was cool and impressive with its big, cold pieces of equipment. He was The Professor. My mother would refer to him, when speaking with others, as "Dr. Hoppmann." She referred to herself as Mrs. Hoppmann. "Mrs. Hoppmann speaking," she would say, when answering the phone, as if to take refuge of some sort in the formality of the phrase, and in the use of my father's name. We were, in fact, a rather formal family.

5   In his work—which was his life—my father dealt with chalk, numbers, and steel. In his laboratory were machines. On his desk was a massive paperweight someone in the Metallurgy Department had given him, a hunk of smoothly ground steel with a cold, precisely cut cross at the top. I liked to heft the weight of it in my hand. I also wondered why anyone would ever admire it, as it was neither beautiful nor inspiring.

6   In the face of my father's demanding personality, my mother seemed to have difficulty holding her own. She was quiet and dutiful, a woman who'd grown up as the fourteenth of sixteen children in a Nebraska farm family. Somewhere along in her sixties, she started—quietly, determinedly—to live her own life, almost in spite of my father. My mother grew tougher and more interesting with age, but when I was growing up she was not tough at all; she was submissive. This same submissiveness was something I saw in virtually every woman I met, growing up—a need to defer to the man who was "taking care of" her, the man on whom she depended for everything.

7   By the time I entered high school I was bringing my ideas home from school—not to Mother, but to Father. There, at the dinner table, he would dissect them with passionate disdain. Then he would move on, digress, go off on a trip of his own that had little to do with me, but always infusing the conversation with great energy. His energy became my energy, or so I thought.

8   My father considered it his God-given duty to point me in the direction of truth—specifically, to correct the mistaken attitudes inflicted upon me by the "third-rate intellects" who were my teachers. His own role as teacher was more fascinating to him by far, I think now, than my fledgling development as a learner. At the age of twelve or thirteen I began to pursue what was to become a lifelong ambition: to get my father to shut up. It was a peculiar, mutual dependence that we had: I wanted his attention;

he wanted mine. He believed that if I would only sit still and listen, he could hand me the world, whole and flawless, like a peeled pear on a silver plate. I didn't want to sit still, and I didn't want the peeled pear. I wanted to find life on my own, in my own way, to stumble upon it like a surprise in a field—the ruddy if misshapen apple that falls from an unpruned tree.

A SECOND LOOK

1. To explain how she gradually lost self-confidence and independence, Dowling describes the differing personalities of her mother and father. Describe in your own words the role model her mother provided.

2. Contrast Dowling's father and mother.

3. When did the conflict between Dowling and her father begin? Describe it.

4. Why, according to Dowling's father, did he force his ideas and attitudes on her? Why did she resent this?

5. A simile is a comparison usually signaled by "like" or "as." In paragraph 8, Dowling uses two similes to explain how her father's attitudes differ from her own. In the first, the world is compared to a peeled pear on a silver platter; in the second, life is compared to a "ruddy if misshapen apple." Contrast the two attitudes that these similes suggest.

6. In what ways might Dr. Hoppmann's profession have contributed to his personality and behavior?

IDEAS FOR WRITING

The title of Dowling's chapter, "Becoming Helpless," suggests that the author's purpose is to analyze the causes that brought about a particular effect, feelings of helplessness and dependency in later life.

Choose an important characteristic of your own personality. Are you shy, fearful, self-confident, studious, religious, and so on? Try to decide what people or places or situations made you the way you are. Make notes as you think about causes and effects in your life. Write down specific details.

You could organize your essay by first describing a particular characteristic. How does it show up in your personality? What difference does it make in your life? Then, in the body of the paper, explain what caused this to be a characteristic of your personality. Describe the cause or causes in detail.

THE GREAT SISTERS AND BROTHERS WAR

Andrew Shanley

LOOKING FORWARD

Andrew Shanley explains that conflict among the children in a family, sibling rivalry, is nearly unavoidable. The fighting can be intense and disturbing, but it usually passes with childhood.

HELP WITH WORDS

writhing *(paragraph 2):* twisting
ensuing *(paragraph 3):* following
cowering *(paragraph 4):* crouching in fear
impassioned *(paragraph 4):* filled with emotion
glowering *(paragraph 7):* looking with anger
banished *(paragraph 11):* made to go
dastardly *(paragraph 11):* mean
dissuade *(paragraph 13):* persuade not to do something

---

1   The evening had been going especially well. As we often do when entertaining guests with children, we fed the kids first so that the adults could have a quiet dinner. All major

events in our lives had just about been covered when our friends'
two boys and our two stormed into the dining room, announced
that it was time for dessert, then raced into the kitchen.

2   I was clearing the dishes when we heard a crash, followed by a
child's howl. We got to the kitchen in time to see our friends'
seven-year-old, Kevin, writhing on the floor and bellowing about
killing his brother, Tod, nine.

3   Physical damage was minimal, but mental anguish was considerable. Apparently there had been an argument over who
would scoop the ice cream. In the ensuing scuffle, Tod had pushed
Kevin to the floor.

4   Now Tod stood cowering in the corner. His mother was giving
him an impassioned lecture.

5   "Don't you realize that if you can't get along with your own
flesh and blood you can't get along with anybody?" she was
asking. "Don't you understand that nobody in the world loves you
more than your brother? And this is how you treat him!"

6   Tod kept his eyes focused on the floor, no doubt wishing he
could be transported to another planet.

7   I looked at Kevin, who was wiping tears from his cheeks and
glowering at his brother like a boxer before the bell signaling the
start of the next round. His father was leaning over and speaking
softly to him.

8   "I'm sure Tod didn't mean it, Kev," he said. "He just got excited
about the ice cream, that's all. The last thing he'd want to do is
hurt you."

9   I wanted Kevin to answer, "Come off it, Dad; he wanted to
knock my head off and you know it!" I was certain I'd smile and
cheer if he did, so I hurried away before his reply.

10   Did our friends really think that siblings should have total
control over their emotions and aggressions? If only Tod's mother
had acknowledged how easy it is to fight with a brother or sister,
then explained it was up to him, the older brother, to show
restraint.

11   As I wiped the dining room table, I thought about my brother,
my sister and I as we were growing up. To call what we experienced sibling rivalry is an understatement; it was more like the
Great Brothers and Sisters War. I remembered the time my
brother and I locked our sister in the closet and "lost" the key—
and the time she hit me with the croquet mallet and fractured my
finger. We were all regulars in solitary—our bedrooms—where

we were banished in an effort to break our urge to commit such dastardly deeds upon one another.

12   We were by no means oddballs among our peer group, either. One friend of mine stuck such a big wad of gum in his sister's beloved shoulder-length hair that it had to be clipped back to her ears. I'm sure she got her revenge, too, though I can't recall how. These wars were never-ending.

13   Siblings know each other's most sensitive buttons as well as when to push them for maximum outrage. Our parents tried every way possible to dissuade us from doing battle, but never told us that fighting with a brother or sister was monstrous and abnormal behavior. Instead, they acknowledged that living together peacefully was difficult, and this was all the more reason to work at it.

14   "You'd better learn to get along," I can hear my mother telling the three of us as if it were yesterday, "because there will be times when all you'll have is each other."

15   I think we somehow understood. Even on those days when we were nastiest to one another, when we swore our grudges would last into eternity, we'd still climb into our beds and talk long after the lights were out. In time, the three of us became the best of friends. In fact, my brother and I each stood as best man at the other's wedding.

16   As parents, we hate to see our children fight. We often feel the blows as if they had landed on us; it hurts to see those we love go against each other. That's natural. But it's important to recognize that problems between sisters and brothers can be part of their competition for our love and attention. And when difficulties do arise, we should make an extra effort to demonstrate our love for them all, possibly focusing it where most needed at that particular moment.

17   When two young boys are diving for the ice cream, however, it's every man for himself with no regard for bloodlines. Later that evening, Tod was playing with our dog when he fell backward over a coffee table onto the floor. He shouted for help. I watched as Kevin ran over and looked down at his brother wedged between the overturned table and the couch.

18   "Got yourself in a bit of a fix, big brother, haven't you?" Kevin asked, smiling and enjoying the moment. Then he reached over to offer Tod a hand. "You owe me," he said, as he pulled the older boy to his feet. "I could have gotten you good."

19   The Great Brothers and Sisters War is often troubling, but as with most wars, it has its own codes, as well as its own cycles. And when the bell sounds for the final round—the one that really counts—our kids usually come out and shake hands.

A SECOND LOOK

1. As many writers do, Shanley captures our attention with an illustration before he states the main idea of his essay. What is his main idea and in which paragraph do you find it?

2. Shanley's sentences often state his ideas with no wasted words. For these economical sentences to work well, they must be carefully structured. What are the patterns of the second sentence in paragraph 1 and the first sentence in paragraph 3?

3. In paragraph 7, Kevin is compared to a boxer, and in paragraphs 11 and 12 the conflicts between brothers and sisters are described as wars. The essay ends with another reference to boxing. Why does Shanley use this exaggeration?

4. The essay ends by returning to Kevin and Tod. Is the dialogue between the two boys in paragraph 18 true to life? Is this what the boys are likely to have said to each other? Is this the language they are likely to have used? Why or why not?

IDEAS FOR WRITING

One way to describe the organization of Shanley's essay is to say that it defines the term *sibling rivalry*. The author uses a detailed illustration and several other examples to explain what sibling rivalry is. He also discusses the characteristics of the rivalry and compares it to fighting and war to make it clear.

Choose a term that you understand thoroughly. It might be a term such as *peer pressure, generation gap, midlife crisis,* or *inferiority complex.* Write an essay in which you try to make the term clear to the reader by giving illustrations and examples of it. What might you compare it to? From what does it differ? Make the term as clear and understandable as possible. Anyone could look up the word in a dictionary, but knowledge from experience will make the term truly understandable. Look at the essays by Marjorie Franco, David Raymond, and Pete Axthelm to see how other writers have developed essays using definition.

MY FAVORITE SISTER

Jennifer Harrison

LOOKING FORWARD

In this student theme, Jennifer Harrison explains how her relationship with her sister changed almost without her realizing it. Somewhat like Sherwood Anderson, she "discovers" someone she has long known.

HELP WITH WORDS

in the limelight *(paragraph 1):* at the center of attention

bewildered *(paragraph 1):* confused

recounts *(paragraph 3):* tells

1 I am the oldest. I am the first child, grandchild, cousin, and niece. This puts me in the position of also being the first to go to school, graduate, get a job, and attend college. I was always in the limelight as a child, and I won't say I didn't love it. But then my sister Laurie was born; she was new and I was "old stuff." I was in the middle of my "terrible twos" that April, and Laurie was very sick right after she was born. Her doctors didn't think she would live through her first week. Mom and Dad were always

worrying and trying to take care of her, and I was totally bewildered because I wasn't the center of attention anymore.

2   I guess I have always been jealous of her because everything she did was "cute." When I did it, the first time, it was an accomplishment. When Laurie did it, she was "cute." Through grade school and up into our junior high years, there was a constant struggle for attention. I strove to do bigger and better things than she could do.

3   We had many, many fights, most of them verbal, but some of varying degrees of violence. The one I remember most was the day she was seven, bouncing on Mom's mattress. I was nine and wise; I ordered her to stop immediately, but she continued her bouncing, then miscalculated the next jump and started falling headfirst toward the floor. I grabbed her arm and pulled her back up onto the bed, but I had jerked her elbow out of its socket, and I got yelled at for "being rough" and "hurting Laurie." To this day, Laurie recounts the story of how "Jenn pulled my whole arm out of its socket," which just plain irritates me.

4   As we grew into our teens, the battles took on new meanings. Fighting over bathroom times, who was using whose shampoo, one of us screeching at the other to get off the phone, and sneaking clothes out of each other's closets were minor wars. Reading each other's letters or diary without permission, sneaking up and scaring each other in the dead of night, and leaving one sister with all the dishes to wash—these were major fights. For some reason, we just couldn't get along at all.

5   We had our last big blowup in early August, a week before I was to leave for college. She was pestering me to get off the telephone so she could call someone, and finally I lost my temper. I yelled, "I can't WAIT until I go to college, 'cause I won't have to listen to you whine anymore!" She screamed right back, "Well, I can't wait 'til you leave, either! I'm looking forward to it!" After a moment of silence to let this all sink in, Laurie said very softly, "Aren't you going to miss me?" I burst into tears because I was already beginning to miss her. We hugged each other, which rarely ever happened, and Mom's eyes bugged out (she had come into the room to split us up).

6   After coming to college I realize that I do miss my sister, and I write to her once a week to keep her up on the latest news. She writes me two or three letters a week and fills me in on all the happenings at our high school. When I call home (collect), Laurie

and I talk for ten to fifteen minutes, or until Dad takes the phone out of her hand. I go home about every other weekend, and we go everywhere together and sit up until late, jabbering. She keeps my room swept and cleaned, and when I went home for Thanksgiving there was a huge, crayoned banner taped to my wall that read, "Welcome Home, Bub!" I loved it. It's like I have found a new friend, somebody who's been there all the time except I didn't know it.

7   It's a little sad that I had to leave home to discover how much I love and miss my sister. I look forward to vacations and summertime, when I'll be with her. After sixteen years of [her] being "The Pest" and "Tag-Along," now I can honestly say my sister is my very best buddy.

A SECOND LOOK

1. Harrison describes a number of experiences with her sister. How does she arrange these to give the theme clear organization?

2. In paragraphs 1 and 4, Harrison is able to pack a lot of information into a small space by the way she puts her sentences together. Analyze the structure of the sentences in these paragraphs.

3. Some readers feel that Harrison's essay would be better if the last paragraph were omitted. Do you agree? Why or why not?

IDEAS FOR WRITING

Complete this sentence: "It is hard for me to be friends with my ____ ." (Fill in the blank with sister, brother, cousin, neighbor, roommate, or the like.) Then write a paragraph beginning with the completed sentence (called a topic sentence). The paragraph should give several reasons for your attitude.

TWO DADS ARE BETTER THAN ONE?

Angela Waugh

LOOKING FORWARD

In this essay written for a freshman composition class, Angela Waugh contrasts her stepfather with her father in order to decide which she should care about more. She hopes that looking at their differences will help her decide what her relationship with them should be.

HELP WITH WORDS

necessities *(paragraph 1):* basic needs
elders *(paragraph 5):* people who are older
objectively *(paragraph 8):* fairly
obligated *(paragraph 9):* bound by a sense of duty

1   I've always envied people with only two parents. They never have to feel sorry for their real father because he is lonely, and they never have to feel they should care more about their stepfather because he is the one who has provided them with the necessities most of their lives.

2   I, since I have two fathers, have known these feelings. I know what it's like trying to decide which father I should care about more so that I could tell my friends the next time they asked.

3   It really should be a clear-cut decision. My two fathers are so different in everything that I should be able to look at these differences and decide.

4   A major difference between the two is how responsible they are. My stepfather has always had a steady job. He enjoys going to work each day and knowing that at the end of the week he'll get a paycheck. With this paycheck he pays bills, buys groceries, and makes sure we all have clothes to wear. On the other hand, my father doesn't particularly care for steady jobs. He is a singer and has worked three or four nights a week in nightclubs most of his life. With his money, he buys things like new guitars and amplifiers. His idea of providing for us, as Mom tells me, is to send ten dollars a month, which is to be divided three ways. He only does this, however, when he's out of state.

5   Discipline is another major difference between my two fathers. My stepfather, who can be very strict at times, believes that children should obey their parents, do what they are told when they are told to do it, and respect their elders. My father, who was never disciplined himself, has quite different views. He has always encouraged my brothers and me to rebel against rules, to ask why we had to do certain things, and to resent being made to do things we thought were stupid. (Going to bed at ten was stupid.) My mother always told us that our father only did this to cause trouble, but I'm not so sure about that. Maybe he did, but then again maybe he thought going to bed at ten was stupid, too!

6   Education is another big issue my stepfather is concerned about. He believes, like many people, that to be able to succeed in life, one has to have a good education. He always told us that he didn't want us to turn out like he did, a truck driver who had to be away from his family for weeks at a time. He used to punish me and my brothers for making C's on our report cards. His theory is that a C is average, and his kids are not average. I wouldn't place any money on that.

7   My father believes that an education is good to have, but one doesn't have to have it to survive. He always says, "Look at me; I made it." I don't think, however, that I would call sleeping in the back of a station wagon "making it"!

8   So here I have it. All their differences down on paper, and I can look at them objectively and decide which father to love more— but it isn't that easy.

9   I love my father because he is just that, my natural father. I respect him; I am obligated to him, and I want to make him proud of me. Then there is my stepfather, whom I respect very much; whom I feel obligated to; whom I want to make proud of me; and, most important of all, whom I have grown to love as much as any child could possibly love a parent.

10   I guess I'll never really know which father I love more. I don't see why I should have to love either more. I think I'll just love both of them in almost equal amounts.

A SECOND LOOK

1. Look again at paragraphs 4–7. Write down a word or phrase that states the main idea of each of these paragraphs. Now check to see what specific information Waugh uses to develop each of these topics.

2. In paragraph 4, what phrase helps Waugh unify her discussion of her two fathers? Are there words, phrases, or sentences that link ideas in other paragraphs?

3. Does Waugh's essay suggest an answer to the question asked by the title?

4. Why do you think Waugh cannot choose between her fathers?

IDEAS FOR WRITING

Do you know two people who are somewhat alike but also different? They might be two friends, two relatives, two teachers, or two roommates. Pick two such people and write an essay showing specifically how they are different.

Begin with one or two paragraphs that introduce your two subjects to the reader. The body of your paper will focus on the differences. Use at least one paragraph to develop each major point with facts, examples, or other supporting details.

MAKING CONNECTIONS

1. Both Sherwood Anderson and Colette Dowling describe fathers who have forceful personalities. Both are dissatisfied with their fathers, but Anderson learns to understand and identify with his father while Dowling feels she must become more and more independent. Which attitude is more common? Do young people most often grow up identifying with or rejecting their fathers? Does the sex of the child make any difference? Does it make a difference that one essay was written in the nineteenth century and the other in the twentieth?

2. Compare the main ideas of Andrew Shanley's "The Great Sisters and Brothers War" and Jennifer Harrison's "My Favorite Sister." Which essay is more effective in explaining sibling rivalry? Why do you think so?

LAUGHTER

AFTER A FALL

Garrison Keillor

LOOKING FORWARD

Laughing at a fall in which no one is hurt is a typical reaction. Garrison Keillor, a writer and comedian, admits that laughing is a natural response, but he then goes on to examine the feelings of the person who has fallen. The victim is likely to view the fall differently. Notice the carefully chosen words that help the reader see the actions Keillor describes.

HELP WITH WORDS

adrenaline *(paragraph 1):* a hormone produced especially in frightening situations

prone *(paragraph 1):* inclined, likely to experience

inexplicable *(paragraph 1):* unexplainable

smirk *(paragraph 3):* a knowing smile

rigorous *(paragraph 3):* demanding

artifacts *(paragraph 3):* man-made objects or tools

perspective *(paragraph 4):* a way of looking at a subject

fundamentalist *(paragraph 14):* one who has religious beliefs based on a literal interpretation of the Bible

constricted *(paragraph 14):* limited

inevitable *(paragraph 14):* unavoidable

nonchalant *(paragraph 15):* unconcerned

1 W hen you happen to step off an edge you didn't see and lurch forward into space waving your arms, it's the end of the world for a second or two, and after you do land, even if you know you're O.K. and no bones are broken it may take a few seconds to decide whether this is funny or not. Your body is still worked up about the fall—especially the nervous system and the adrenaline-producing areas. In fact, I am still a little shaky from a spill that occurred two hours ago, when I put on a jacket, walked out the front door of this house here in St. Paul, Minnesota, and for no reason whatever took a plunge down five steps and landed on the sidewalk flat on my back with my legs in the air. I am thirty-nine years old and in fairly good shape, not prone to black-outs or sudden dizziness, and so a sudden inexplicable fall comes as a big surprise to me.

2 A woman who was jogging down the street—a short, muscular young woman in a gray sweatshirt and sweatpants— stopped and asked if I was O.K. "Yeah! Fine!" I said and got right up. "I just fell, I guess," I said. "Thanks," I said. She smiled and trotted away.

3 Her smile has followed me into the house, and I see it now as a smirk, which is what it was. She was too polite to bend over and hoot and shriek and guffaw and cackle and cough and whoop and wheeze and slap her thighs and stomp on the ground, but it was there in that smile: a young woman who through rigorous physical training and feminist thinking has gradually been taking charge of her own life and ridding her attic of self-hatred and doubt and fear and mindless competitiveness and other artifacts of male-dominated culture is rewarded with the sight of a middle-aged man in a brown suit with a striped tie falling down some steps as if someone had kicked him in the pants.

4 I'm sorry if I don't consider this humorous. I would like to. I wish she had come over and helped me up and then perhaps sat on the steps with me while I calmed down. We might have got to talking about the fall and how each of us viewed it from a different perspective. . . .

5 I might have seen it her way, but she ran down the street, and now I can only see my side of the fall. I feel old and achy and ridiculous and cheapened by the whole experience. I understand now why my son was so angry with me a few months ago when he tripped on a shoelace and fell in the neighbor's yard—a yard where the neighbor's sheepdog had lived for years—and I cackled at him.

6   "It's not funny!" he yelled.

7   "Oh, don't be so sensitive," I said.

8   Don't be so sensitive! What a dumb thing to say! Who has the right to tell someone else how to feel? It is the right of the person who falls in the dog droppings to decide for himself or herself how he or she will feel. It's not up to a jury. The fallen person determines whether it's funny or not. . . .

9   Five years ago, I got on a bus with five musicians and rode around for two weeks doing shows every night. They played music; I told jokes and sang a song. One night, in the cafeteria of a junior college in southern Minnesota, we happened to draw a big crowd, and the stage—four big plywood sheets on three-foot steel legs—was moved back twenty feet to make room for more chairs. The show was late starting, the room was stuffy, the crowd was impatient, and when finally the lights dimmed and the spotlight shone on the plywood, I broke from the back door and made a run for the stage, thinking to make a dramatic entrance and give these fine people the show they were waiting for.

10   What I could not see in the dark was the ceiling and a low concrete overhang that the stage had been moved partly under, and then the spotlight caught me straight in the eyes and I couldn't see anything. I leaped up onto the stage, and in mid-leap my head hit concrete and my right leg caught the plywood at mid-shin. I toppled forward, stuck out my hands, and landed on my hands and knees. The crowd drew a long breath. I got right up—I had been doing shows long enough to know not to lie onstage and cry in front of a paying audience—and, seeing the microphone about ten feet ahead, strode up to it and held out my arms and said, "Hello, everybody! I'm happy to be here!"

11   Then they laughed—a big thunderstorm of a laugh and a big round of applause for what they now saw had been a wonderful trick. But it wasn't funny! My neck hurt! I hurt all over! On the other hand, to see a tall man in a white suit jump directly into a ceiling and then fall down—how often does a person get to see that? Men dive off high towers through fiery hoops into tiny tanks, men rev up motorcycles and leap long rows of trucks and buses, but I am the only man in show business who takes a good run and jumps Straight Up Into Solid Concrete Using Only His Bare Head. Amazing! . . .

12   Oh, it is a sad story, except for the fact that it isn't. My ceiling jump got the show off to a great start. The band played three fast

tunes, and I jumped carefully back onstage and did a monologue that the audience, which now knew I was funny, laughed at a lot. Even I, who had a headache, thought it was funny. I really did feel lucky.

13 So do I still—a tall man who fell now sitting down to write his memoirs. The body is so delicate, the skeleton so skinny; we are stick men pencilled in lightly, with a wooden stick cage to protect the heart and lungs and a cap of bone over the brain. I wonder that I have survived so many plunges, so many quick drops down the short arc that leads to the ground. . . .

14 The first time I ever went naked in mixed company was at the house of a girl whose father had a bad back and had built himself a sauna in the corner of the basement. Donna and I were friends in college. Both of us had grown up in fundamentalist Christian homes, and we liked to compare notes on that. We both felt constricted by our upbringings and were intent on liberating ourselves and becoming more free and open and natural. So it seemed natural and inevitable one night to wind up at her house with some of her friends there and her parents gone and to take off our clothes and have a sauna.

15 We were nineteen years old and were very cool ("Take off my clothes? Well, sure. Heck, I've taken them off dozens of times") and were careful to keep cool and be nonchalant and not look at anybody below the neck. We got into the sauna as if getting on the bus. People do this, I thought to myself. There is nothing unusual about it! Nothing! We all have bodies! There is no reason to get excited! This is a normal part of life!

16 We filed into the little wooden room, all six of us, avoiding unnecessary body contact, and Donna poured a bucket of water on the hot rocks to make steam. It was very quiet. "There's a shower there on the wall if you want to take a shower," she said in a strange, nervous voice.

17 "Hey! How about a shower!" a guy said in a cool-guy voice, and he turned on the water full blast. The shower head leaped from the wall. It was a hand-held type—a nozzle at the end of a hose—and it jumped out at us like a snake and thrashed around exploding ice-cold water. He fell back, someone screamed, I slipped and fell, Donna fell on top of me, we leaped apart, and meanwhile the nozzle danced and flew from the force of the blast of water. Donna ran out of the sauna and slipped and fell on the laundry-room floor, and another girl yelled, "God damn you,

Tom!" Donna scrambled to her feet. "God! Oh, God!" she cried. Tom yelled, "I'm sorry!" Another guy laughed a loud, wicked laugh, and I tiptoed out as fast as I could move, grabbed my clothes, and got dressed. Donna grabbed her clothes. "Are you all right?" I said, not looking at her or anything. "No!" she said. Somebody laughed a warm, appreciative laugh from inside the sauna. "Don't laugh!" she yelled. "It isn't funny! Is isn't the least bit funny!"

18   "I'm not laughing," I said, though it wasn't me she was angry at. I still am not laughing. I think it's a very serious matter, twenty years later. Your first venture as a naked person, you want it to go right and be a good experience, and then some joker has to go pull a fast one. . . .

19   I haven't seen you since that night, Donna. I've told the sauna story to dozens of people over the years, and they all thought it was funny but I still don't know what you think. Are you all right?

A SECOND LOOK

1. Keillor opens the essay with a personal experience. In what paragraph does he state the main idea of the essay? What is it?

2. In paragraph 3, Keillor chooses unusual verbs to describe the way he imagines the woman would like to laugh at him. Explain why the description is amusing.

3. What does Keillor mean when he says in paragraph 3 that the woman's smile "followed me into the house"?

4. Look carefully at the way Keillor tells about his experience in the sauna. Describe some of the techniques that make the story amusing.

5. Why does Keillor end the essay with a question addressed to Donna? Why does he ask this particular question?

IDEAS FOR WRITING

1. Most people could add to Garrison Keillor's essay examples of funny or embarrassing falls they have had. In a paragraph or two, tell

about some spill you have taken. Explain how it happened and what you looked like. Work especially on using detailed description that will help the reader imagine the actions. The test for success in this paper is whether the reader can see what you describe.

2. Victims of falls are like victims of jokes: They are expected to laugh at themselves and think no more about it. Have you ever been the butt of a joke that was funny to everyone except you? Write an essay in which you describe the joke and then explain your reaction to it. Try to make the reader understand your side of the story.

CHICKEN GIZZARDS

James A. Perkins

LOOKING FORWARD

"Chicken Gizzards" is about a humorous experience remembered from childhood. In this sketch, James Perkins—a teacher and the author of short stories, poems, and radio and TV scripts—makes a point about the joy of competition as well as the joy of eating gizzards.

HELP WITH WORDS

flanked *(paragraph 1):* placed at the sides

din *(paragraph 4):* a loud noise

strategy *(paragraph 5):* a plan for achieving a specific result

visions *(paragraph 5):* persons or events seen only in the mind

spiel *(paragraph 5):* a sales pitch

groused *(paragraph 7):* complained

---

1 Daddy and his daddy, Pap, and daddy's brother-in-law, Uncle Eddie, all loved to eat. Whenever our family got together it was around a table, a table loaded with food. I always hoped for ham, but their favorite was fried chicken, and there was usually a heaping platter of fried chicken flanked by steaming bowls of green beans and mashed potatoes and gravy.

2   Besides liking chicken, they all three liked the gizzard best of all, and down underneath of those wings and drumsticks and thighs and whatnot was the one gizzard. I think it all started one Sunday when Pap picked up the platter, smiled sheepishly and said, "Would any of y'all like this here chicken craw?" "Don't mind if I do," said Daddy, and he forked the gizzard right off the platter. Pap's eyes went hard. He just sat there holding that empty platter with both hands. Finally he set it down and said, "I see." From then on we all saw that it was war, and it lasted for years.

3   At first it was rather crude. Daddy took a wing and passed the chicken to Uncle Eddie. He slid the back off the platter and casually swept the gizzard with it. I could tell by the way they looked at him when he set the empty platter down that he had broken the rules and the last easy victory had been won.

4   Piece by piece another Sunday's chicken was eaten, and the three of them finally sat there staring at the gizzard. When Pap's wife, Lucy, asked, "One of you going to eat that thing?" she was ignored. Finally Pap made his move. There was an awful din of clashing metal and screaming. Pap forked the gizzard. Daddy, like an old time sheriff letting the hired gun slap leather first, nailed that gizzard to the platter with a fork, and Uncle Eddie, who, being right-handed, was at a disadvantage having to reach across, stuck his fork in the back of Pap's hand.

5   It was about then that strategy was introduced. "My Gawd. It looks like Fronk's barn's on fire," yelled Pap. Daddy and Uncle Eddie didn't see any fire out the window. When they turned back they didn't see any gizzard either, and Pap was laughing so hard he nearly choked on it. After that there were so many visions that you would have thought we were a family of Roman Catholics instead of dyed-in-the-wool, dull-as-paint Presbyterians. Pap saw things out the window. Daddy saw things out the back door. Uncle Eddie, who sat facing the china cupboard, was again at somewhat of a disadvantage. One time he told about the woman selling Bibles door to door, whose panties fell off right in the middle of the sales spiel, and gobbled the gizzard whole while Pap and Daddy were laughing. Another time he just sat there staring up at the ceiling. That didn't work. Pap said, "You can't treat us like a bunch of green horns at the county fair. That ceiling's been up there since the house was built, and I ain't taking my eyes off that gizzard."

6   Toward the end nobody believed anybody or anything. One Sunday afternoon the fire bell rang and the three of them just sat there staring at the gizzard, each of them convinced that one of the other two had paid Curly Beckett to ring the bell.

7   It all came to an end on a Thanksgiving. They hunted all morning and came in to a big chicken dinner. When all the wings and legs and whatnot were gone, there on the platter were three gizzards. "Mr. Macklin gave them to me extra when I bought the chicken," said Lucy. They ignored her. They just sat there sullenly looking at those three gizzards. Pap finally forked one of them and groused, "Who the Hell ever heard of a chicken havin' three gizzards?"

A SECOND LOOK

1. Words that appeal to the five senses make writing more lively. Which of the senses are appealed to by the description in paragraph 1? Look at other paragraphs to find sense words.

2. Daddy, Pap, and Uncle Eddie have various tricks for getting the gizzard. List them in the order in which they occur in the sketch. Why does the author use this order?

3. Lucy tries to be helpful by cooking three gizzards for Thanksgiving, but her help is not appreciated. What does she fail to understand?

IDEAS FOR WRITING

1. Make a list of a dozen or so sights that are pleasant to you. Look over the list to see whether there is a pattern. Try to draw a generalization about sights that please you. (For example, "I enjoy looking at scenes that remind me of fall in my home town," or "I like to see things around me that make my room cozy and comfortable," or "I like to look at strange and unfamiliar places.") Then go through the same process for the other senses: hearing, smell, taste, and touch. In each case, make a generalization from the list.

   For the writing assignment, write three paragraphs using three of the generalizations as topic sentences. Develop the paragraphs by using details from the lists. Each paragraph should be about fifty words long. Note that these are three separate paragraphs; they should not be related to each other.

2. Describe for a group of classmates a humorous incident that occurred at a family gathering. Begin by jotting down all the details you remember about the incident. Next, select only those details that will help your readers understand what made this occurrence funny to you. When you begin writing the description, be sure the introduction makes clear when the incident happened and who was involved.

SEX ED—
THE PROS AND CONS

Art Buchwald

LOOKING FORWARD

Art Buchwald is well known for writing about serious topics in a humorous way. His subjects are often political issues, but here his topic is more personal: He explains how he learned the "facts of life."

HELP WITH WORDS

ultraconservatives *(paragraph 1):* people who are strongly opposed to change

John Birchers *(paragraph 1):* members of the John Birch Society, an ultraconservative organization

DAR *(paragraph 1):* Daughters of the American Revolution, a politically conservative organization for descendants of Revolutionary soldiers

dispensed *(paragraph 3):* distributed

rumble seat *(paragraph 4):* an open-air seat built into the back of old-model cars where the trunk now is

canards *(paragraph 6):* false stories

horrendous *(paragraph 9):* horrible

indoctrination *(paragraph 11):* instruction in a particular set of ideas

awe *(paragraph 11):* deep respect

1   There is a big flap going on in the United States right now over the question of teaching sex education in our schools. The educators are mostly for it and the ultraconservatives, including the John Birchers and the DAR, are mostly against it. I usually like to stay out of controversial matters since I hate to answer my mail, but in this case I have to come out for teaching sex education in the schools.

2   This is a very personal matter with me. I had no formal sex education when I was a student, and everyone knows the mess I'm in. If there had been a Head Start program in sex education when I was going to public school, I might have been a different man today.

3   When I was going to Public School 35 in Hollis, New York, we got all our sex education at the local candy store after three o'clock. The information was dispensed by thirteen-year-olds who seemed to know everything there was to know on the subject, and we eleven- and twelve-year-olds believed every word they told us.

4   Some of it, I discovered later on, did not necessarily happen to be true. For example, I was told as an absolute fact that if a girl necked with you in the rumble seat of a car, she would automatically have a baby.

5   This kept me out of the rumble seat of an automobile until I was twenty-three years old.

6   There were some other canards of the day, including one that the method of kissing a girl on the mouth decided whether she would become pregnant or not. Every time I kissed a girl after that, I sweated for the next nine months.

7   The sex experts at Sam's Candy Store had an answer for every problem that was raised at the soda fountain. These included warnings that if you did certain things, you would go insane. Most of us were prepared to be taken off to the booby hatch at any moment.

8   There was obviously no talk about birds, bees, flowers, or animals. We couldn't care less what happened when they were doing it. Our only concern was what happened to human beings, and from what our thirteen-year-old instructors could tell us, it was all bad.

9   Those of us who escaped insanity and shotgun weddings were told we would probably wind up with a horrendous disease that would be passed on to our children and their children for genera-

tions to come. There were twenty-five ways of catching this disease, including shaking hands with someone who knew someone who had it.

10   You can imagine the nightmares these tales produced. There seemed to be no escape. You were doomed if you did, and you were doomed if you didn't. After one of these sessions at the candy store, I seriously contemplated suicide. There didn't seem to be any other way out.

11   Now the worst part of my sex indoctrination was that when I turned thirteen, I became an instructor myself and passed on my knowledge to eleven- and twelve-year-olds at the same candy store. They listened in awe as I repeated word for word what I had been told by my "teachers," and I was amazed with how much authority I was able to pass on the "facts" of sex education as I knew them.

12   Upon becoming thirteen, they in turn taught the younger students. Heaven knows how many generations of Public School 35 alumni went on through life believing everything they had learned about sex at Sam's Candy Store.

13   The fact is that while the sex education at Sam's served a purpose, we were all emotional wrecks before we got to high school.

14   So, on the basis of my own experience, I don't think we have much choice in this country when it comes to sex education. In order to avoid the agony and pain my fellow classmates and I went through, we either have to teach sex in the schools or close down every soda fountain in the United States.

A SECOND LOOK

1. What sort of eleven-year-old was Buchwald? Why does he stress this point early in the essay?

2. Pick out several of the pieces of misinformation given out at the candy store. Are these misunderstandings typical or unusual?

3. What does Buchwald consider the greatest advantage of teaching sex education in the schools?

IDEAS FOR WRITING

Nearly all children and adolescents get confused or pick up false information as they are growing up. Sometimes the result is funny; sometimes it can be frightening. Did you ever misunderstand something or believe incorrect information that got you into either a humorous or an unpleasant situation? (Some topics about which young people are often confused are sex, religion, sports, relationships with parents, and relationships with peers.) If you can remember such a misunderstanding, write a short paper about it. Your readers will want clear answers to three questions:

1. What were you confused about, or what kind of wrong information did you have?

2. What did you do based on this misinformation?

3. What was the result?

You can organize your paper by following the order of the questions.

THE FIRST KISS

Steven Graves

LOOKING FORWARD

In this freshman essay, a student remembers an important event in his life. Notice that the amused attitude is that of the mature Steven Graves looking back, not that of young Stevie Graves, the first-grader being described.

HELP WITH WORDS

burr-headed *(paragraph 1):* having a short haircut

incredible *(paragraph 1):* unbelievable

virile *(paragraph 2):* manly

knickers *(paragraph 4):* knee-length pants

---

1   Of parades and circus trips and all those anxiously awaited jaunts to Grandmother's or the ice cream parlor, the most memorable occasion of all was my first kiss. The electricity that went through my body and soul was enough to light Manhattan. Every hair on my burr-headed little body stood on end. The nights afterward weren't long enough to handle the incredible dreams that rushed through my head.

2   There I was, Stevie Graves, "Peaches" to my friends, young and virile, finely tuned body, masculine approach to problems,

and sporting one of the most beautiful flattops in the first grade at Ewing Elementary School. My uncle, who was older, a fourth grader, had explained the process of the first kiss to me, and I was ready. He went on to explain more, but I decided I would perfect one thing at a time.

3   Now I'm not saying I didn't already have a grasp of kissing. My mother and dad never kissed when I could see them, but my cousin Jane was all lips. She and her boyfriend used to kiss for hours and hours, even days. I thought they were going to die from lack of air once. I couldn't see much except lips through that keyhole, but that was enough to cause strange feelings in me.

4   I had been in love with a girl named Debbie ever since I started kindergarten, and I knew that when the moment was just right, she was going to be the one. And she was. There I stood, grammar book in one hand, a copy of *Daisy the Cow* in the other, and my knickers bound tight around my knees. No, that's a lie. I never had knickers, but my stance on the front steps of the school that day must have looked very noble anyway.

5   We had been writing to each other for months about getting together for a kiss or two, but now it was going to happen. Here she came off the bus, bouncing like a basketball, hair in braids, teeth in braces, just bursting with youth and excitement, ready for—yes, the kiss. She ran towards me, and I knew it was now. She passed me by, but then she turned, ran back, and planted the most beautiful kiss right on my cheek. I was electric, caught at the top of the ferris wheel of first-grade sexual response.

6   As years passed, I forgot about Debbie, but that kiss will always be a place, a time, an experience I'll never forget. If only I could be there again, waiting anxiously to be swept off my feet by a gentle peck on the cheek.

A SECOND LOOK

1. How does the author create humor in this essay?

2. The essay is not as loosely organized as it first appears to be. Briefly outline the organization.

3. Pick out several descriptive words or phrases and explain why you consider them to be effective. Pay particular attention to paragraph 5.

IDEAS FOR WRITING

1. Tell about an emotion-filled experience from your elementary-school days. This kind of paper needs careful organization. Begin by indicating the subject (such as a first kiss) and setting up the situation. Then tell about the event itself. Be sure the action is described in the order in which it occurred. If you wish, you may close by looking back from the present and commenting on this past emotional experience.

2. In a paragraph, describe yourself as a first-grader. Include details about your appearance and your feelings. Your description may be completely factual or, like Steven Graves's self-portrait, it may include slight humorous exaggeration.

MAKING CONNECTIONS

Reconsider the essays in this unit to decide which of them use humor to make a serious point. Decide what point is made in each case. Why is humor sometimes an effective way to communicate serious ideas?

DIFFERENCES

ON BEING SEVENTEEN, BRIGHT, AND UNABLE TO READ

David Raymond

LOOKING FORWARD

David Raymond's difference is his inability to read—not because of any lack of training, but because of dyslexia. This condition, which prevents an individual from recognizing words and sometimes even numbers, results from a brain dysfunction. As Raymond's title suggests, dyslexia is unrelated to intelligence. Notice that Raymond opens with a specific example, then introduces his main idea in paragraph 2.

HELP WITH WORDS

facilities *(paragraph 14):* places or equipment designed for special purposes

1 One day a substitute teacher picked me to read aloud from the textbook. When I told her, "No, thank you," she came unhinged. She thought I was acting smart, and told me so. I kept calm, and that got her madder and madder. We must have

spent ten minutes trying to solve the problem, and finally she got so red in the face I thought she'd blow up. She told me she'd see me after class.

2   Maybe someone like me was a new thing for that teacher. But she wasn't new to me. I've been through scenes like that all my life. You see, even though I'm seventeen and a junior in high school, I can't read because I have dyslexia. I'm told I read "at a fourth-grade level," but from where I sit, that's not reading. You can't know what that means unless you've been there. It's not easy to tell how it feels when you can't read your homework assignments or the newspaper or a menu in a restaurant or even notes from your own friends.

3   My family began to suspect I was having problems almost from the first day I started school. My father says my early years in school were the worst years of his life. They weren't so good for me, either. As I look back on it now, I can't find the words to express how bad it really was. I wanted to die. I'd come home from school screaming, "I'm dumb. I'm dumb—I wish I were dead!"

4   I guess I couldn't read anything at all then—not even my own name—and they tell me I didn't talk as good as other kids. But what I remember about those days is that I couldn't throw a ball where it was supposed to go, I couldn't learn to swim, and I wouldn't learn to ride a bike, because no matter what anyone told me, I knew I'd fail.

5   Sometimes my teachers would try to be encouraging. When I couldn't read the words on the board they'd say, "Come on, David, you know that word." Only I didn't. And it was embarrassing. I just felt dumb. And dumb was how the kids treated me. They'd make fun of me every chance they got, asking me to spell "cat" or something like that. Even if I knew how to spell it, I wouldn't; they'd only give me another word. Anyway, it was awful, because more than anything I wanted friends. On my birthday when I blew out the candles I didn't wish I could learn to read; what I wished for was that the kids would like me.

6   With the bad reports coming from school, and with me moaning about wanting to die and how everybody hated me, my parents began looking for help. That's when the testing started. The school tested me, the child guidance center tested me, private psychiatrists tested me. Everybody knew something was wrong—especially me.

7   It didn't help much when they stuck a fancy name onto it. I couldn't pronounce it then —I was only in second grade—and I was ashamed to talk about it. Now it rolls off my tongue, because I've been living with it for a lot of years—dyslexia.

8   All through elementary school it wasn't easy. I was always having to do things that were "different," things the other kids didn't have to do. I had to go to a child psychiatrist, for instance.

9   One summer my family forced me to go to a camp for children with reading problems. I hated the idea, but the camp turned out pretty good, and I had a good time. I met a lot of kids who couldn't read and somehow that helped. The director of the camp said I had a higher IQ than 90 percent of the population. I didn't believe him.

10   About the worst thing I had to do in fifth and sixth grade was go to a special education class in another school in our town. A bus picked me up, and I didn't like that at all. The bus also picked up emotionally disturbed kids and retarded kids. It was like going to a school for the retarded. I always worried that someone I knew would see me on that bus. It was a relief to go to the regular junior high school.

11   Life began to change a little for me then, because I began to feel better about myself. I found the teachers cared; they had meetings about me and I worked harder for them for a while. I began to work on the potter's wheel, making vases and pots that the teachers said were pretty good. Also, I got a letter for being on the track team. I could always run pretty fast.

12   At high school the teachers are good and everyone is trying to help me. I've gotten honors some marking periods and I've won a letter on the cross-country team. Next quarter I think the school might hold a show of my pottery. I've got some friends. But there are still some embarrassing times. For instance, every time there is writing in the class, I get up and go to the special education room. Kids ask me where I go all the time. Sometimes I say, "To Mars."

13   Homework is a real problem. During free periods in school I go into the special ed room and staff members read assignments to me. When I get home my mother reads to me. Sometimes she reads an assignment into a tape recorder and then I go into my room and listen to it. If we have a novel or something like that to read, she reads it out loud to me. Then I sit down with her and we

do the assignment. She'll write, while I talk my answers to her. Lately, I've taken to dictating into a tape recorder, and then someone—my father, a private tutor or my mother—types up what I've dictated. Whatever homework I do takes someone else's time, too. That makes me feel bad.

14 We had a big meeting in school the other day—eight of us, four from the guidance department, my private tutor, my parents and me. The subject was me. I said I wanted to go to college, and they told me about colleges that have facilities and staff to handle people like me. That's nice to hear.

15 As for what happens after college, I don't know and I'm worried about that. How can I make a living if I can't read? Who will hire me? How will I fill out the application form?

16 The only thing that gives me any courage is the fact that I've learned about well-known people who couldn't read or had other problems and still made it. Like Albert Einstein, who didn't talk until he was four and flunked math. Like Leonardo da Vinci, who everyone seems to think had dyslexia.

17 I've told this story because maybe some teacher will read it and go easy on a kid in the classroom who has what I've got. Or maybe some parent will stop nagging his kid, and stop calling him lazy. Maybe he's not lazy or dumb. Maybe he just can't read and doesn't know what's wrong. Maybe he's scared, like I was.

A SECOND LOOK

1. Besides the inability to read, what were some other early signs of David Raymond's dyslexia?

2. Mention several changes that helped Raymond to feel better about himself.

3. Raymond often uses casual words or even slang—for example, "thought she'd blow up" (paragraph 1). Find other examples of this type of language. What impression does this language create?

4. Raymond uses many details from his personal experience. How does he put them in order?

5. In general, this essay explains what has happened to the writer and how he feels about it. The last paragraph, however, serves a different purpose. What is it?

IDEAS FOR WRITING

1. Think of a time when you felt different from those around you. What was the difference? Did you look different or talk differently? Could everyone else do something that you could not? As exactly as you can, remember the situation, and recall how you reacted. Were you embarrassed, angry, hurt, or all of these?

   Now write an essay in which you first describe the time when you felt different, then explain why you felt as you did. Finally, tell how you reacted. You will be writing, as David Raymond did, for a group of readers who do not know you.

2. One way of defining something is to explain how it works. David Raymond helps to explain what dyslexia is by showing how it affected his life. If you know of some condition like dyslexia that has made a difference in your life or the life of someone you know, help to define or explain that condition by showing its effects. You may begin, as Raymond did, with an example, or you may begin by mentioning the condition. Your readers may be familiar with the condition you are explaining, but they do not know you or the person you are writing about.

I'D RATHER BE BLACK THAN FEMALE

Shirley Chisholm

LOOKING FORWARD

Shirley Chisholm has been a nursery school teacher and director, an educational consultant, a New York State Assembly member, and, of course, a United States congresswoman. She is also an active lecturer and writer. The differences that former Congresswoman Chisholm discusses are those that stir up racial and sexual prejudices. Readers may be surprised at Chisholm's statement that it is easier to deal with racism than with sexism.

HELP WITH WORDS

phenomenon *(paragraph 1):* something out of the ordinary

bizarre *(paragraph 2):* odd, very unusual

incredulous *(paragraph 3):* unbelieving

tedious *(paragraph 5):* without change

dashikis *(paragraph 9):* bright, colorful pullover shirts that originated in Africa

tokenism *(paragraph 11):* admitting small numbers of minorities into a group for the sake of appearances

menial *(paragraph 11):* degrading

vocation *(paragraph 14):* job

empathy *(paragraph 17):* feeling what another person feels

persistence *(paragraph 17):* determination

---

1   Being the first black woman elected to Congress has made me some kind of phenomenon. There are nine other blacks in Congress; there are ten other women. I was the first to overcome both handicaps at once. Of the two handicaps, being black is much less of a drawback than being female.

2   If I said that being black is a greater handicap than being a woman, probably no one would question me. Why? Because "we all know" there is prejudice against black people in America. That there is prejudice against women is an idea that still strikes nearly all men—and, I'm afraid, most women—as bizarre.

3   Prejudice against blacks was invisible to most white Americans for many years. When blacks finally started to "mention" it, with sit-ins, boycotts, and freedom rides, Americans were incredulous. "Who, us?" they asked in injured tones. "We're prejudiced?" It was the start of a long, painful reeducation for white America. It will take years for whites—including those who think of themselves as liberals—to discover and eliminate the racist attitudes they all actually have.

4   How much harder will it be to eliminate the prejudice against women? I am sure it will be a longer struggle. Part of the problem is that women in America are much more brainwashed and content with their roles as second-class citizens than blacks ever were.

5   Let me explain. I have been active in politics for more than twenty years. For all but the last six, I have done the work—all the tedious details that make the difference between victory and defeat on election day—while men reaped the rewards, which is almost invariably the lot of women in politics.

6   It is still women—about 3 million volunteers—who do most of this work in the American political world. The best any of them can hope for is the honor of being district or county vice-chairman, a kind of separate-but-equal position with which a woman is rewarded for years of faithful envelope stuffing and

card-party organizing. In such a job, she gets a number of free trips to state and sometimes national meetings and conventions, where her role is supposed to be to vote the way her male chairman votes.

7   When I tried to break out of that role in 1963 and run for the New York State Assembly seat from Brooklyn's Bedford-Stuyvesant, the resistance was bitter. From the start of that campaign, I faced undisguised hostility because of my sex.

8   But it was four years later, when I ran for Congress, that the question of my sex became a major issue. Among members of my own party, closed meetings were held to discuss ways of stopping me.

9   My opponent, the famous civil rights leader James Farmer, tried to project a black, masculine image; he toured the neighborhood with sound trucks filled with young men wearing Afro haircuts, dashikis, and beards. While the television crews ignored me, they were not aware of a very important statistic, which both I and my campaign manager, Wesley MacD. Holder, knew. In my district there are two and a half women for every man registered to vote. And those women are organized—in PTA's, church societies, card clubs, and other social and service groups. I went to them and asked their help. Mr. Farmer still doesn't quite know what hit him.

10   When a bright young woman graduate starts looking for a job, why is the first question always: "Can you type?" A history of prejudice lies behind that question. Why are women thought of as secretaries, not administrators? Librarians and teachers, but not doctors and lawyers? Because they are thought of as different and inferior. The happy homemaker and the contented darky are both stereotypes produced by prejudice.

11   Women have not even reached the level of tokenism that blacks are reaching. No women sit on the Supreme Court. Only two have held Cabinet rank, and none do at present. Only two women hold ambassadorial rank. But women predominate in the lower-paying, menial, unrewarding, dead-end jobs, and when they do reach better positions, they are invariably paid less than a man gets for the same job.

12   If that is not prejudice, what would you call it?

13   A few years ago, I was talking with a political leader about a promising young woman as a candidate. "Why invest time and effort to build the girl up?" he asked me. "You know she'll only

drop out of the game to have a couple of kids just about the time we're ready to run her for mayor."

14   Plenty of people have said similar things about me. Plenty of others have advised me, every time I tried to take another upward step, that I should go back to teaching, a woman's vocation, and leave politics to the men. I love teaching, and I am ready to go back to it as soon as I am convinced that this country no longer needs a woman's contribution.

15   When there are no children going to bed hungry in this rich nation, I may be ready to go back to teaching. When there is a good school for every child, I may be ready. When we do not spend our wealth on hardware to murder people, when we no longer tolerate prejudice against minorities, and when the laws against unfair housing and unfair employment practices are enforced instead of evaded, then there may be nothing more for me to do in politics.

16   But until that happens—and we all know it will not be this year or next—what we need is more women in politics, because we have a very special contribution to make. I hope that the example of my success will convince other women to get into politics—and not just to stuff envelopes, but to run for office.

17   It is women who can bring empathy, tolerance, insight, patience, and persistence to government—the qualities we naturally have or have had to develop because of our suppression by men. The women of a nation mold its morals, its religion, and its politics by the lives they live. At present, our country needs women's idealism and determination, perhaps more in politics than anywhere else.

A SECOND LOOK

1. According to Shirley Chisholm, why is it easier to be black than to be female?

2. Chisholm's audience is clearly different from David Raymond's. What difference does this fact make in her word choice and sentence structure? Look for specific examples.

3. Part of Chisholm's purpose is to persuade her readers, to convince them to agree with her view. What are some of the ways she tries to do this?

4. Look at paragraph 11. Since this was written, a woman has been appointed to the Supreme Court, and several more women have held cabinet posts. Do these facts weaken Chisholm's main point? Have the conditions mentioned in paragraph 15 changed?

IDEAS FOR WRITING

1. In paragraph 10, Chisholm talks about stereotypes. (If you are not familiar with this word, check your dictionary.) People often stereotype others according to their sex, race, religion, economic status, or even the area where they live. Have you ever been stereotyped or unfairly labeled? Describe this experience for your classmates, explaining what happened and how you felt. Begin by writing down everything you can remember about the experience. Then go back and cross out details that seem unimportant. Now relate the experience so that your readers will understand exactly what happened and how you reacted.

2. Reread Chisholm's last paragraph. Does she also stereotype? If you believe she does, write her a letter in which you try to convince her that women and men both may have one of the qualities she mentions: empathy, tolerance, insight, patience, or persistence. Even though you are not writing an essay, your letter can be a type of persuasive writing.

HALFWAY TO DICK AND JANE

Jack Agueros

LOOKING FORWARD

The son of Puerto Rican immigrants, Jack Agueros grew up in Spanish Harlem. The differences he writes about are caused by both passing time and varying ethnic backgrounds.

HELP WITH WORDS

dismantle *(paragraph 2):* take apart

plantain *(paragraph 2):* a large plant with leaves and fruit similar to the banana

compensation *(paragraph 2):* payment

foyer *(paragraph 2):* entrance hall

declaim *(paragraph 2):* recite dramatically

immaculate *(paragraph 3):* spotlessly clean

railroad flat *(paragraph 5):* a narrow apartment with the rooms connecting in a single line and with doors front and back

intensified *(paragraph 7):* made stronger

pathetically *(paragraph 7):* very sadly

pathologically *(paragraph 7):* in an unhealthy or diseased way

1   I am an only child. My parents and I always talked about my becoming a doctor. The law and politics were not highly regarded in my house. Lawyers, my mother would explain, had to defend people whether they were guilty or not, while politicians, my father would say, were all crooks. A doctor helped everybody, rich and poor, white and black. If I became a doctor, I could study hay fever and find a cure for it, my godmother would say. Also, I could take care of my parents when they were old. I liked the idea of helping, and for nineteen years my sole ambition was to study medicine.

2   My house had books, not many, but my parents encouraged me to read. As I became a good reader they bought books for me and never refused me money for their purchase. My father once built a bookcase for me. It was an important moment, for I had always believed that my father was not too happy about my being a bookworm. The atmosphere at home was always warm. We seemed to be a popular family. We entertained frequently, with two standing parties a year—at Christmas and for my birthday. Parties were always large. My father would dismantle the beds and move all the furniture so that the full two rooms could be used for dancing. My mother would cook up a storm, particularly at Christmas. *Pasteles, lechon asado, arroz con gandules,* and a lot of *coquito* to drink (meat-stuffed plantain, roast pork, rice with pigeon peas, and coconut nog). My father always brought in a band. They played without compensation and were guests at the party. They ate and drank and danced while a victrola covered the intermissions. One year my father brought home a whole pig and hung it in the foyer doorway. He and my mother prepared it by rubbing it down with oil, oregano, and garlic. After preparation, the pig was taken down and carried over to a local bakery where it was cooked and returned home. Parties always went on till daybreak, and in addition to the band, there were always volunteers to sing and declaim poetry.

3   My mother kept an immaculate household. Bedspreads (chenille seemed to be very in) and lace curtains, washed at home like everything else, were hung up on huge racks with rows of tight nails. The racks were assembled in the living room, and the moisture from the wet bedspreads would fill the apartment. In a sense, that seems to be the lasting image of that period of my life. The house was clean. The neighbors were clean. The streets, with

few cars, were clean. The buildings were clean and uncluttered with people on the stoops. The park was clean. The visitors to my house were clean, and the relationships that my family had with other Puerto Rican families, and the Italian families that my father had met through baseball and my mother through the garment center, were clean. Second Avenue was clean and most of the apartment windows had awnings. There was always music, there seemed to be no rain, and snow did not become slush. School was fun, we wrote essays about how grand America was, we put up hunchbacked cats at Halloween, we believed Santa Claus visited everyone. I believed everyone was Catholic. I grew up with dogs, nightingales, my godmother's guitar, rocking chair, cat, guppies, my father's occasional roosters, kept in a cage on the fire escape. Laundry delivered and collected by horse and wagon, fruits and vegetables sold the same way, windowsill refrigeration in winter, iceman and box in summer. The police my friends, likewise the teachers.

4   In short, the first seven or so years of my life were not too great a variation on Dick and Jane, the school book figures who, if my memory serves me correctly, were blond Anglo-Saxons, not immigrants, not migrants like the Puerto Ricans, and not the children of either immigrants or migrants.

5   My family moved in 1941 to Lexington Avenue into a larger apartment where I could have my own room. It was a light, sunny, railroad flat on the top floor of a well-kept building. I transferred to a new school, and whereas before my classmates had been mostly black, the new school had few blacks. The classes were made up of Italians, Irish, Jews, and a sprinkling of Puerto Ricans. My block was populated by Jews, Italians, and Puerto Ricans.

6   And then a whole series of different events began. I went to junior high school. We played in the backyards, where we tore down fences to build fires to cook stolen potatoes. We tore up whole hedges, because the green tender limbs would not burn when they were peeled, and thus made perfect skewers for our stolen "mickies." We played tag in the abandoned buildings, tearing the plaster off the walls, tearing the wire lath off the wooden slats, tearing the wooden slats themselves, good for fires, for kites, for sword fighting. We ran up and down the fire escapes playing tag and over and across many rooftops. The war ended

and the heavy Puerto Rican migration began. The Irish and the Jews disappeared from the neighborhood. The Italians tried to consolidate east of Third Avenue.

7   What caused the clean and open world to end? Many things. Into an ancient neighborhood came pouring four to five times more people than it had been designed to hold. Men who came running at the promise of jobs were jobless as the war ended. They were confused. They could not see the economic forces that ruled their lives as they drank beer on the corners, reassuring themselves of good times to come while they were hell-bent toward alcoholism. The sudden surge in numbers caused new resentments, and prejudice was intensified. Some were forced to live in cellars, and were then characterized as cave dwellers. Kids came who were confused by the new surroundings; their Puerto Ricanness forced us against a mirror asking, "If they are Puerto Ricans, what are we?" and thus they confused us. In our confusion we were sometimes pathetically reaching out, sometimes pathologically striking out. Gangs. Drugs. Wine. Smoking. Girls. Dances and slow-drag music. Mambo. Spics, Spooks, and Wops. Territories, brother gangs, and war councils establishing rules for right of way on blocks and avenues and for seating in the local theater. Pegged pants and zip guns. Slang.

8   Dick and Jane were dead, man. Education collapsed. Every classroom had ten kids who spoke no English. Black, Italian, Puerto Rican relations in the classroom were good, but we all knew we couldn't visit one another's neighborhoods. Sometimes we could not move too freely within our own blocks. On 109th, from the lamp post west, the Latin Aces, and from the lamp post east, the Senecas, the "club" I belonged to. The kids who spoke no English became known as Marine Tigers, picked up from a popular Spanish song. (The Marine Tiger and the Marine Shark were two ships that sailed from San Juan to New York and brought over many, many migrants from the island.)

9   The neighborhood had its boundaries. Third Avenue and east, Italian. Fifth Avenue and west, black. South, there was a hill on 103rd Street known locally as Cooney's Hill. When you got to the top of the hill, something strange happened: America began, because from the hill south was where the "Americans" lived. Dick and Jane were not dead: they were alive and well in a better neighborhood.

10   When, as a group of Puerto Rican kids, we decided to go swimming to Jefferson Park Pool, we knew we risked a fight and a beating from the Italians. And when we went to La Milagrosa Church in Harlem, we knew we risked a fight and a beating from the blacks. But when we went over Cooney's Hill, we risked dirty looks, disapproving looks, and questions from the police like, "What are you doing in this neighborhood?" and "Why don't you kids go back where you belong?"

11   Where we belonged! Man, I had written compositions about America. Didn't I belong on the Central Park tennis courts, even if I didn't know how to play? Couldn't I watch Dick play? Weren't these policemen working for me too? . . .

A SECOND LOOK

1. Dick and Jane were the white, middle-class characters in a series of reading textbooks once very popular in lower elementary school. What does Agueros mean by "Halfway to Dick and Jane"? What does he mean when he refers to the characters again in paragraphs 8, 9, and 11?

2. What differences occur after Agueros moves to Lexington Avenue? What are the causes of these differences?

3. Agueros says that when new immigrant kids moved into the neighborhood, "their Puerto Ricanness forced us against a mirror asking, 'If they are Puerto Ricans, what are we?'" What does he mean by this?

4. Beginning in paragraph 7 there are some changes in the author's style, especially in his word choice and sentence structure. What are these changes and why do you think he makes them?

5. If you have read the selection from Maxine Hong Kingston's *The Woman Warrior*, compare her experience with that of Jack Agueros. How were their childhoods similar and how were they different? Do you think Kingston, as she is described in this selection, would describe herself as "halfway to Dick and Jane"? Explain why or why not.

IDEAS FOR WRITING

1. If you are the child of immigrant parents (or perhaps if you know well someone else who is), then you too may understand what it is like to be caught between two cultures. If so, describe this feeling.

   Explain how it feels to move away from one culture and toward another. You might consider such questions as these: Do you feel good or bad about this experience? Are you moving voluntarily from one culture to another, or do you feel you are being forced? Do you resent either cultural group or perhaps both? What are the advantages and disadvantages of the move? Use specific details and brief descriptions of specific experiences to show your readers how you feel. Assume that your readers are of various ethnic or cultural backgrounds; that is, they are not all Hispanic, all black, all white, and so on.

2. A policeman says to Agueros and his friends: "Why don't you kids go back where you belong?" Has anyone ever made you feel as if you didn't belong? If so, describe that experience. Tell your readers what the situation was, who said you did not belong, and how you reacted to that charge.

3. Have you ever lived in a neighborhood or a community that went through a major change, growing either better or worse? If so, write about the experience. Explain to your readers (who may not be familiar with the place you are describing) how the place was before the change and then after. Also explain the reasons the change occurred. (You may wish to look again at paragraphs 5–9 of "Halfway to Dick and Jane.")

HARRISON BERGERON

Kurt Vonnegut, Jr.

LOOKING FORWARD

Kurt Vonnegut, Jr., has been popular, especially with college-age readers, for a number of years. He has written many essays and short stories, in addition to such well-known novels as *Slaughterhouse Five* and *Breakfast of Champions*. In "Harrison Bergeron," a science fiction short story, Vonnegut imagines a future society in which all differences have been outlawed and the government is responsible for making everyone equal. Consider whether the government has completely succeeded and whether or not such equality is desirable.

HELP WITH WORDS

unceasing vigilance *(paragraph 1):* endless watchfulness

sashweights *(paragraph 10):* weights used for raising and lowering windows

winced *(paragraph 11):* moved unwillingly, as from pain

glimmeringly *(paragraph 21):* faintly

impediment *(paragraph 37):* handicap

luminous *(paragraph 41):* bright, glowing

grackle *(paragraph 42):* a bird with a harsh call

calibrated *(paragraph 43):* measured off

symmetry *(paragraph 45):* balance or order

consternation *(paragraph 49):* concern

cowered *(paragraph 53):* knelt fearfully

capered, gamboled *(paragraph 73):* leaped, skipped

---

1   T he year was 2081, and everybody was finally equal. They weren't only equal before God and the law. They were equal in every which way. Nobody was smarter than anybody else. Nobody was better looking than anybody else. Nobody was stronger or quicker than anybody else. All this equality was due to the 211th, 212th, and 213th Amendments to the Constitution, and to the unceasing vigilance of agents of the United States Handicapper General.

2   Some things about living still weren't quite right, though. April, for instance, still drove people crazy by not being springtime. And it was in that clammy month that the H-G men took George and Hazel Bergeron's fourteen-year-old son, Harrison, away.

3   It was tragic, all right, but George and Hazel couldn't think about it very hard. Hazel had a perfectly average intelligence, which meant she couldn't think about anything except in short bursts. And George, while his intelligence was way above normal, had a little mental handicap radio in his ear. He was required by law to wear it at all times. It was tuned to a government transmitter. Every twenty seconds or so, the transmitter would send out some sharp noise to keep people like George from taking unfair advantage of their brains.

4   George and Hazel were watching television. There were tears on Hazel's cheeks, but she'd forgotten for the moment what they were about.

5   On the television screen were ballerinas.

6   A buzzer sounded in George's head. His thoughts fled in panic, like bandits from a burglar alarm.

7   "That was a real pretty dance, that dance they just did," said Hazel.

8   "Huh?" said George.

9   "That dance—it was nice," said Hazel.

10   "Yup," said George. He tried to think a little about the ballerinas. They weren't really very good—no better than anybody else

would have been anyway. They were burdened with sashweights and bags of birdshot, and their faces were masked, so that no one, seeing a free and graceful gesture or a pretty face, would feel like something the cat drug in. George was toying with the vague notion that maybe dancers shouldn't be handicapped. But he didn't get very far with it before another noise in his ear radio scattered his thoughts.

11   George winced. So did two out of the eight ballerinas.

12   Hazel saw him wince. Having no mental handicap herself, she had to ask George what the latest sound had been.

13   "Sounded like somebody hitting a milk bottle with a ball peen hammer," said George.

14   "I'd think it would be real interesting, hearing all the different sounds," said Hazel, a little envious. "All the things they think up."

15   "Um," said George.

16   "Only, if I was Handicapper General, you know what I would do?" said Hazel. Hazel, as a matter of fact, bore a strong resemblance to the Handicapper General, a woman named Diana Moon Glampers. "If I was Diana Moon Glampers," said Hazel, "I'd have chimes on Sunday—just chimes. Kind of in honor of religion."

17   "I could think, if it was just chimes," said George.

18   "Well—maybe make 'em real loud," said Hazel. "I think I'd make a good Handicapper General."

19   "Good as anybody else," said George.

20   "Who knows better'n I do what normal is?" said Hazel.

21   "Right," said George. He began to think glimmeringly about his abnormal son who was now in jail, about Harrison, but a twenty-one-gun salute in his head stopped that.

22   "Boy!" said Hazel, "that was a doozy, wasn't it?"

23   It was such a doozy that George was white and trembling, and tears stood on the rims of his red eyes. Two of the eight ballerinas had collapsed to the studio floor, were holding their temples.

24   "All of a sudden you look so tired," said Hazel. "Why don't you stretch out on the sofa, so's you can rest your handicap bag on the pillows, honeybunch." She was referring to the forty-seven pounds of birdshot in a canvas bag, which was padlocked around George's neck. "Go on and rest the bag for a little while," she said. "I don't care if you're not equal to me for a while."

25   George weighed the bag with his hands. "I don't mind it," he said. "I don't notice it any more. It's just a part of me."

26   "You've been so tired lately—kind of wore out," said Hazel. "If there was just some way we could make a little hole in the bottom of the bag, and just take out a few of them lead balls, just a few."

27   "Two years in prison and two thousand dollars fine for every ball I took out," said George. "I don't call that a bargain."

28   "If you could just take a few out when you came home from work," said Hazel. "I mean—you don't compete with anybody around here. You just set around."

29   "If I tried to get away with it," said George, "then other people'd get away with it—and pretty soon we'd be right back to the dark ages again, with everybody competing against everybody else. You wouldn't like that, would you?"

30   "I'd hate it," said Hazel.

31   "There you are," said George. "The minute people start cheating on laws, what do you think happens to society?"

32   If Hazel hadn't been able to come up with an answer to this question, George couldn't have supplied one. A siren was going off in his head.

33   "Reckon it'd fall all apart," said Hazel.

34   "What would?" said George blankly.

35   "Society," said Hazel uncertainly. "Wasn't that what you just said?"

36   "Who knows?" said George.

37   The television program was suddenly interrupted for a news bulletin. It wasn't clear at first as to what the bulletin was about, since the announcer, like all announcers, had a serious speech impediment. For about half a minute, and in a state of high excitement, the announcer tried to say, "Ladies and gentlemen—"

38   He finally gave up, handed the bulletin to a ballerina to read.

39   "That's all right—" Hazel said to the announcer, "he tried. That's the big thing. He tried to do the best he could with what God gave him. He should get a nice raise for trying so hard."

40   "Ladies and gentlemen—" said the ballerina, reading the bulletin. She must have been extraordinarily beautiful because the mask she wore was hideous. And it was easy to see that she was the strongest and most graceful of all the dancers, for her handicap bags were as big as those worn by two-hundred-pound men.

41   And she had to apologize at once for her voice, which was a very unfair voice for a woman to use. Her voice was warm, luminous, timeless, melody. "Excuse me—" she said, and she began again, making her voice absolutely uncompetitive.

42   "Harrison Bergeron, age fourteen," she said in a grackle squawk, "has just escaped from jail, where he was held on suspicion of plotting to overthrow the government. He is a genius and an athlete, is underhandicapped, and should be regarded as extremely dangerous."

43   A police photograph of Harrison Bergeron was flashed on the screen upside down, then sideways, upside down again, then right side up. The picture showed the full length of Harrison against a background calibrated in feet and inches. He was exactly seven feet tall.

44   The rest of Harrison's appearance was Halloween and hardware. Nobody had ever borne heavier handicaps. He had outgrown hindrances faster than the H-G men could think them up. Instead of a little ear radio for a mental handicap, he wore a tremendous pair of earphones, and spectacles with thick wavy lenses. The spectacles were intended to make him not only half blind, but to give him whanging headaches besides.

45   Scrap metal was hung all over him. Ordinarily, there was a certain symmetry, a military neatness to the handicaps issued to strong people, but Harrison looked like a walking junkyard. In the race of life, Harrison carried three hundred pounds.

46   And to offset his good looks, the H-G men required that he wear at all times a red rubber ball for a nose, keep his eyebrows shaved off, and cover his even white teeth with black caps at snaggletooth random.

47   "If you see this boy," said the ballerina, "do not—I repeat, do not—try to reason with him."

48   There was the shriek of a door being torn from its hinges.

49   Screams and barking cries of consternation came from the television set. The photograph of Harrison Bergeron on the screen jumped again and again, as though dancing to the tune of an earthquake.

50   George Bergeron correctly identified the earthquake, and well he might have—for many was the time his own home had danced to the same crashing tune. "My God—" said George, "that must be Harrison!"

51   The realization was blasted from his mind instantly by the sound of an automobile collision in his head.

52   When George could open his eyes again, the photograph of Harrison was gone. A living, breathing Harrison filled the screen.

53   Clanking, clownish, and huge, Harrison stood in the center of

the studio. The knob of the uprooted studio door was still in his hand. Ballerinas, technicians, musicians, and announcers cowered on their knees before him, expecting to die.

54 "I am the Emperor!" cried Harrison. "Do you hear? I am the Emperor! Everybody must do what I say at once!" He stamped his foot and the studio shook.

55 "Even as I stand here—" he bellowed, "crippled, hobbled, sickened—I am a greater ruler than any man who ever lived! Now watch me become what I *can* become!"

56 Harrison tore the straps of his handicap harness like wet tissue paper, tore straps guaranteed to support five thousand pounds.

57 Harrison's scrap-iron handicaps crashed to the floor.

58 Harrison thrust his thumbs under the bar of the padlock that secured his head harness. The bar snapped like celery. Harrison smashed his headphones and spectacles against the wall.

59 He flung away his rubber-ball nose, revealed a man that would have awed Thor, the god of thunder.

60 "I shall now select my Empress!" he said, looking down on the cowering people. "Let the first woman who dares rise to her feet claim her mate and her throne!"

61 A moment passed, and then a ballerina arose, swaying like a willow.

62 Harrison plucked the mental handicap from her ear, snapped off her physical handicaps with marvelous delicacy. Last of all, he removed her mask.

63 She was blindingly beautiful.

64 "Now—" said Harrison, taking her hand, "shall we show the people the meaning of the word dance? Music!" he commanded.

65 The musicians scrambled back into their chairs, and Harrison stripped them of their handicaps, too. "Play your best," he told them, "and I'll make you barons and dukes and earls."

66 The music began. It was normal at first—cheap, silly, false. But Harrison snatched two musicians from their chairs, waved them like batons as he sang the music as he wanted it played. He slammed them back into their chairs.

67 The music began again and was much improved.

68 Harrison and his Empress merely listened to the music for a while—listened gravely, as though synchronizing their heartbeats with it.

69 They shifted their weights to their toes.

70 Harrison placed his big hand on the girl's tiny waist, letting her sense the weightlessness that would soon be hers.

71 And then, in an explosion of joy and grace, into the air they sprang!

72 Not only were the laws of the land abandoned, but the law of gravity and the laws of motion as well.

73 They reeled, whirled, swiveled, flounced, capered, gamboled, and spun.

74 They leaped like deer on the moon.

75 The studio ceiling was thirty feet high, but each leap brought the dancers nearer to it.

76 It became their obvious intention to kiss the ceiling.

77 They kissed it.

78 And then, neutralizing gravity with love and pure will, they remained suspended in air inches below the ceiling, and they kissed each other for a long, long time.

79 It was then that Diana Moon Glampers, the Handicapper General, came into the studio with a double-barreled 10-gauge shotgun. She fired twice, and the Emperor and the Empress were dead before they hit the floor.

80 Diana Moon Glampers loaded the gun again. She aimed it at the musicians and told them they had ten seconds to get their handicaps back on.

81 It was then that the Bergeron's television tube burned out.

82 Hazel turned to comment about the blackout to George. But George had gone out into the kitchen for a can of beer.

83 George came back in with the beer, paused while a handicap signal shook him up. And then he sat down again. "You been crying?" he said to Hazel.

84 "Yup," she said.

85 "What about?" he said.

86 "I forget," she said. "Something real sad on television."

87 "What was it?" he said.

88 "It's all kind of mixed up in my mind," said Hazel.

89 "Forget sad things," said George.

90 "I always do," said Hazel.

91 "That's my girl," said George. He winced. There was the sound of a riveting gun in his head.

92 "Gee—I could tell that one was a doozy," said Hazel.

93 "You can say that again," said George.

94 "Gee—" said Hazel, "I could tell that one was a doozy."

A SECOND LOOK

1. How are George and Hazel different from each other?

2. Describe the kinds of handicaps George has been given.

3. In paragraph 14 we learn that Hazel is "a little envious." Why? What does this suggest about the plan for universal equality?

4. How is Diana Moon Glampers, the Handicapper General, different from everyone else in the story?

5. Vonnegut certainly does not believe that such "equality" is good. Point out several places where he suggests that this idea is unworkable.

6. What words in paragraphs 69–71 suggest movement? Why is movement so important at this point in the story?

7. Define equality, as Vonnegut describes it in the story. What is your definition of the term?

IDEAS FOR WRITING

1. Reread paragraphs 66–79, which describe the scene in the TV studio just as the Handicapper General arrives and then her response to that scene. Try to imagine this action from the Handicapper General's point of view. Write a brief, factual report from the Handicapper General to the President, explaining (from her point of view) what was occurring and what action she had to take.

2. Imagine how some one part of society or one type of common experience may differ in 2081. You might choose law enforcement, marriage, factory work, teaching and learning, or any activity about which your imagination can roam. If your instructor wishes, you might brainstorm in small groups of three or four. In your brainstorming session, think of as many details as possible about the way your activity will be carried out in 2081. Then select those that are most interesting or that best go together to make a complete description. (You may do this individually, or, if you are working in groups, you may discuss your list with others.)

   When you write, you may assume that you are in the present predicting what the future will be like. In that case, you will write in the future tense. On the other hand, you could assume that you are already in the future and are describing what it is like. In that case, you will write in the present tense. (You might try the first paragraph both ways and see which you prefer.)

MAKING CONNECTIONS

David Raymond, Shirley Chisholm, and Jack Agueros write about differences that, when emphasized, made them feel lonely or angry or discriminated against. Vonnegut presents differences as important and desirable. Do differences among people have a positive effect on society? When and how do differences cause social problems?

SPORTS

HOW TO PLAY
SECOND BASE

Laurence Sheehan

LOOKING FORWARD

Although Laurence Sheehan's title suggests that this essay gives instructions on playing second base, that is not the main idea. Instead, the author writes in a humorous way about the value of playing ball, even for a youngster without much talent.

HELP WITH WORDS

ill-fated *(paragraph 2):* having bad luck

demoralized *(paragraph 3):* discouraged

humiliation *(paragraph 3):* disgrace

consecutive *(paragraph 4):* one after the other

The Thumper *(paragraph 5):* Ted Williams

taunts *(paragraph 8):* insults

extinction *(paragraph 13):* complete destruction

sieve *(paragraph 14):* strainer

indifference *(paragraph 15):* lack of concern

avenge *(paragraph 16):* to get even, especially for someone else

1   S econd base is the most important position in baseball. Nobody realizes. A lot of coaches don't even bother to tell their second basemen the first thing about the job. They don't think second base is worth the effort.

2   The unfortunate name of second base is partly to blame. It just sounds like a hand-me-down. I think the ill-fated manager Joe McCarthy of the Boston Red Sox also once said something like second base is neither first nor third. That was the situation when I was playing for Centerville School, and I doubt if it's improved much since then, not at Centerville or in the majors.

3   Why is second base so important? Because when an easy grounder or a high pop-up is hit to that position, and you kick it away, or misjudge it and let it bounce on your head, the whole team gets demoralized. The shortstop comes over and says, "Too bad the school bus didn't clip you this morning." The first base-man slaps his leg and laughs. The pitcher gives you the finger in front of everybody. Of course there may not be that many people at the game, so the public humiliation won't count for much. Centerville hardly ever drew a crowd because it was always in the last place in its division, thanks in part to slight miscalcula-tions by the second baseman.

4   I got my little sister Evie to come a lot when games were played at Legion Field in our neighborhood. But she didn't understand baseball. She would see me strike out on three consecutive pitch-es, or get run through by a steaming grounder. But she wouldn't find such happenings interesting enough to report to our parents. I'd have to tell them myself at supper.

5   You might say that for Evie my baseball failings went in one eye and out the other. She was a lousy fan. I sometimes wondered why I had her come to the games at all, which I did starting when I made the team in the sixth grade and got my uniform. I don't think she even knew what number I wore (9—The Thumper's own!). Anyway, if it weren't for the bubble gum my black pal Herman kept giving her, she probably would have stopped com-ing long before she finally did. Herman played third. She would chew gum or eat an apple or orange from home, and watch out that no one stole our gloves when we were at bat, but basically Evie paid no attention to what was going on. She usually sat on the opposing team's bench, to my great embarrassment. It was closer to the water fountain.

6   Back to second base now. There are tips that can make anybody play this position better and I'd like to pass them along.

7   By the way, I didn't mean to imply I minded my teammates' groaning and hooting at my errors. I mean I minded, but I understood. And basically we had a close-knit infield. It wasn't any dream infield, such as the Bosox built around the great Bobby Doerr and Johnny Pesky in the same years I was at Centerville, but we had a pretty good team feeling. Erwin, our regular pitcher, would put up with four or five errors in one inning before going to the finger. Lover Boy, the first baseman, would laugh at errors and kid a lot, but actually he didn't care where the ball went or even who won. His mind was always on his girlfriends who were waiting for him up in the nearly empty stands. Bert, our team captain at short, would come over after I'd let one go through my legs and say, "All right, let's get back in this game now." And of course Herman, who never made an error himself over at third, would not get upset by anything I did. Or anybody did. He was the coolest cucumber on the squad.

8   Not even State Street's Butch Mendoza, the division's Home Run King and number one razzer, could get through to Herman. We had no regular coaches on the bases. Older players on each team did the job. Mendoza liked to do it for State Street. He'd coach first base and rib Lover Boy about his shaggy hair and his white cleats, and Lover Boy would nod and smile, probably not even hearing Butch's taunts, too busy dreaming about those girls of his up in the stands and about his plans for them all after the game. When Butch coached third he liked to rib Herman about his color. "Hey, boy, where's your watermelon today?" he'd say, or "How come you're not picking cotton this week?" At that time blacks were few and far between in our town, no matter what grammar school you went to, and Butch probably thought of Herman as a foreigner. The important thing is, Herman paid no attention to Butch and never did make an error before his eyes.

9   I'll spare the outfielders on Centerville. Like most outfielders they were hotshots, and I suppose because they managed to get more hits and runs than anybody else, they had a right to parade around out there and editorialize on every move the infielders made.

10   Now then, the hardest play to handle is the infield fly. I say anytime a ball goes higher than it goes farther, it is going to be a

son of a gun to catch. In my playing days, half of the time I wouldn't even know when one of those high pops was entering my territory. I'd need to hear Lover Boy call over, "Hey, little man, here comes trouble!"

11   Anyway, you've got to get set. A good thing is to get your feet in motion. And bend your neck back far enough so your eyes see more than the brim of the baseball cap. Everything about school uniforms is fine except the brims on the caps. They are made for adult heads, and if you stand four feet three and weigh seventy-five pounds, the hat will be like an awning on your forehead. The only thing you'll be able to see without any strain is your feet, which as I said should be in motion anyway—as you commence dancing into position to make a stab at the catch.

12   Of course, once you get your head tilted back far enough so you can see past the brim of your cap, you risk being temporarily blinded by the sun. Even on cloudy days it is possible for the sun to come out just at the crucial instant and make you lose sight of the damn ball, assuming you ever saw it in the first place. . . .

13   Covering the bag properly is another important duty. I never had much practice taking throws from the catcher, to put out base stealers, because in such cases the Centerville catchers either threw the ball way into the outfield or hit poor Erwin with it as he tried to get out of the way. I did handle throws from the outfield a lot. Naturally our outfielders had to show off their powerful throwing arms so, on an attempted double, say, I would face two means of extinction: (1) breaking my hand on the hard throw from the field, or (2) getting run over from behind by the base runner.

14   Actually I never got spiked or knocked down by runners, but there were many close calls. By far the most dangerous man on base in the division was Butch Mendoza, as you might have guessed by what I've mentioned about him already. Once Butch knocked Herman on his ass coming into third. Right away we had to bring in a young kid at Herman's position who was almost as bad as I was out there. I remember Lover Boy saying, "My, my, we are now fielding a hole at second and a sieve at third!"

15   Herman was nowhere near the base and Butch should have been called out for running outside his normal course. He deliberately picked Herman off because of Herman's color and maybe even more because of Herman's indifference to Butch's many

taunts. He should have been called out, but even the umpires were afraid of Butch Mendoza in those days. He was three times Herman's height and twice his weight, I'd guess. So Herman got carted off by Bert and Erwin and me, wind knocked out of him, and as it turned out, one arm busted.

16   In the meantime, I remember, Evie got up from the State Street bench, where she was sitting, naturally, and hit Butch with what was left of the apple she'd been chomping on. Got him in the face with her apple core after he'd crossed home plate. She turned and ran toward home and Butch was too surprised and out of breath anyway to do much about it. He just looked confused. I felt like catching up with Evie and buying her a Popsicle for trying to avenge Herman as she had done. I guess I knew, even as I helped cart off Herman, who was chewing his bubble gum like crazy at the time, to keep from crying probably—I guess I knew Butch had done something he would be ashamed of in later years, provided he ever stopped to think about it. And little Evie had done something she'd never stop to think about, because she was at that age when you can deal with villains cleanly.

17   In any case I couldn't have walked out on Centerville even though we were losing about twelve to three at the time. We got Herman settled down and took the field again and finished the last two or three innings. I think State Street got a couple more runs off us, to rub it in. We never got on base again, but that didn't make any difference—we stuck it out. That's really about the last thing I wanted to pass along about the job of playing second base, whether you're winning or losing, or making five errors per game, or seeing one of your teammates get a bad break, or losing your only fan. Stick it out. That's what second base is all about.

A SECOND LOOK

1. Sheehan appears to ramble, but he really jumps from one subject to another on purpose. What does he discuss in paragraphs 5, 7, 8, 16, and 17?

2. Sheehan says his sister Evie "was a lousy fan." What details does he give to support his statement? When Evie hits Butch with the apple core, Sheehan is pleased with her. Why?

3. In paragraph 15, Sheehan says that Butch Mendoza knocked Herman down mostly "because of Herman's indifference to Butch's many taunts." Explain this.

4. Why does young Sheehan continue to play for a team that is always last in its division?

5. Like Serwood Anderson in "Discovery of a Father," Sheehan often sounds more as if he were talking to you than writing to you. Look closely at paragraphs 5, 6, and 7. How does the author create the informal sound of telling a story? Find other examples.

IDEAS FOR WRITING

1. In brief paragraphs, describe young Laurence, Butch, and Herman. Try not to use the same words the author uses.

2. One of Sheehan's major ideas is that it is sometimes important to continue doing something even if you do not do it well. Write a paper in which you agree or disagree. Your main idea will be that something (you decide what) is or is not worthwhile for its own sake. First think of that "something." Then give several reasons to show that it is or is not worth doing. Arrange your reasons either from most to least important or from least to most important; do not just put them in random order. At the end of your essay, you should return to the main idea you stated at the beginning.

SEND YOUR CHILDREN TO THE LIBRARIES

Arthur Ashe

LOOKING FORWARD

Arthur Ashe played professional tennis for a number of years, winning many awards. He was outstanding in both Wimbledon and Davis Cup competition. But in this letter published in *The New York Times*, Ashe argues that there are actually few opportunities in professional sports for black athletes. He suggests that there are many roles in society, besides those in sports, that blacks can and should fill.

HELP WITH WORDS

pretentious *(paragraph 2):* falsely superior

expends *(paragraph 3):* spends

dubious *(paragraph 3):* questionable

emulate *(paragraph 4):* follow or imitate

massive *(paragraph 6):* very large

viable *(paragraph 9):* workable

channel *(paragraph 12):* direct

1 Since my sophomore year at University of California, Los Angeles, I have become convinced that we blacks spend too much time on the playing fields and too little time in the libraries.

2 Please don't think of this attitude as being pretentious just because I am a black, single, professional athlete.

3 I don't have children, but I can make observations. I strongly believe the black culture expends too much time, energy and effort raising, praising and teasing our black children as to the dubious glories of professional sports.

4 All children need models to emulate—parents, relatives or friends. But when the child starts school, the influence of the parent is shared by teachers and classmates, by the lure of books, movies, ministers and newspapers, but most of all by television.

5 Which televised events have the greatest number of viewers? Sports—the Olympics, Super Bowl, Masters, World Series, pro basketball playoffs, Forest Hills. ABC-TV even has sports on Monday night prime time from April to December.

6 So your child gets a massive dose of O. J. Simpson, Kareem Abdul-Jabbar, Muhammad Ali, Reggie Jackson, Dr. J. and Lee Elder and other pro athletes. And it is only natural that your child will dream of being a pro athlete himself.

7 But consider these facts: For the major professional sports of hockey, football, basketball, baseball, golf, tennis and boxing, there are roughly only 3,170 major league positions available (attributing 200 positions to golf, 200 to tennis and 100 to boxing). And the annual turnover is small.

8 We blacks are a subculture of about 28 million. Of the 13½ million men, 5–6 million are under twenty years of age, so your son has less than once chance in a thousand of becoming a pro. Less than one in a thousand. Would you bet your son's future on something with odds of 999 to 1 against you? I wouldn't.

9 Unless a child is exceptionally gifted, you should know by the time he enters high school whether he has a future as an athlete. But what is more important is what happens if he doesn't graduate or doesn't land a college scholarship and doesn't have a viable alternative job career. Our high school dropout rate is several times the national average, which contributes to our unemployment rate of roughly twice the national average.

10 And how do you fight the figures in the newspapers every day?

Ali has earned more than $30 million boxing, O. J. just signed for $2½ million, Dr. J for almost $3 million, Reggie Jackson for $2.8 million, Nate Archibald for $400,000 a year. All that money, recognition, attention, free cars, girls, jobs in the off-season—no wonder there is Pop Warner football, Little League baseball, National Junior League tennis, hockey practice at 5 A.M. and pickup basketball games in any center city at any hour.

11   There must be some way to assure that the 999 who try but don't make it to pro sports don't wind up on the street corners or in the unemployment lines. Unfortunately, our most widely recognized role models are athletes and entertainers—"runnin'" and "jumpin'" and "singin'" and "dancin'." While we are 60 percent of the National Basketball Association, we are less than 4 percent of the doctors and lawyers. While we are about 35 percent of major league baseball, we are less than 2 percent of the engineers. While we are about 40 percent of the National Football League, we are less than 11 percent of construction workers such as carpenters and bricklayers.

12   Our greatest heroes of the century have been athletes—Jack Johnson, Joe Louis and Muhammad Ali. Racial and economic discrimination forced us to channel our energies into athletics and entertainment. These were the ways out of the ghetto, the ways to that Cadillac, those alligator shoes, that cashmere sport coat.

13   Somehow, parents must instill a desire for learning alongside the desire to be Walt Frazier. Why not start by sending black professional athletes to high schools to explain the facts of life.

14   I have often addressed high school audiences and my message is always the same. For every hour you spend on the athletic field, spend two in the library. Even if you make it as a pro athlete, your career will be over by the time you are thirty-five. So you will need that diploma.

15   Have these pro athletes explain what happens if you break a leg, get a sore arm, have one bad year or don't make the cut for five or six tournaments. Explain to them the star system, wherein for every O. J. earning millions there are six or seven others making $15,000 or $20,000 or $30,000 a year.

16   But don't just have Walt Frazier or O. J. or Abdul-Jabbar address your class. Invite a benchwarmer or a guy who didn't make it. Ask him if he sleeps every night. Ask him whether he

was graduated. Ask him what he would do if he became disabled tomorrow. Ask him where his old high school athletic buddies are.

17   We have been on the same roads—sports and entertainment—too long. We need to pull over, fill up at the library and speed away to Congress and the Supreme Court, the unions and the business world. We need more Barbara Jordans, Andrew Youngs, union cardholders, Nikki Giovannis and Earl Graveses. Don't worry: We will still be able to sing and dance and run and jump better than anybody else.

18   I'll never forget how proud my grandmother was when I graduated from UCLA in 1966. Never mind the Davis Cup in 1968, 1969, and 1970. Never mind the Wimbledon title, Forest Hills, etc. To this day, she still doesn't know what those names mean.

19   What mattered to her was that of her more than thirty children and grandchildren, I was the first to be graduated from college, and a famous college at that. Somehow, that made up for all those floors she scrubbed all those years.

A SECOND LOOK

1. In this letter, Ashe uses many statistics. Are they convincing? Why or why not?

2. What evidence besides statistics does he use to support his main idea?

3. Ashe says, "We have been on the same roads—sports and entertainment—too long." Does he mean that blacks should avoid these careers?

4. Ashe's audience consists of parents of black sons. Could his argument apply to other races or to parents of girls? Why or why not?

5. The best piece of evidence to strengthen Ashe's argument may be Ashe himself. How does the letter show this?

IDEAS FOR WRITING

Write a letter to the editor in which you state an opinion that you feel strongly about. Begin by stating the opinion clearly in a single sentence. Decide who your readers will be. Are you writing for a campus newspaper? A community newspaper? A big-city daily?

Next, write down all the reasons you can think of why your readers should accept your opinion. Decide which are most effective and then begin to organize your letter. Begin with your statement of opinion. Follow with support. Near the end, restate the opinion, though not in the same words you used at the beginning.

BASKETBALL PLAYER

John Updike

LOOKING FORWARD

Poet, novelist, and short story writer John Updike has often written about former athletes, like Flick Webb in this poem. In the poem, Updike shows how Flick's life has changed by describing him at work and after work. Pay special attention to Flick's feelings about his past.

HELP WITH WORDS

tiers *(line 29):* rows rising one behind the other, as in bleachers

Necco Wafers, Nibs, and Juju Beads *(line 30):* brands of candy and snacks

---

Pearl Avenue runs past the high school lot,
Bends with the trolley tracks, and stops, cut off
Before it has a chance to go two blocks,
At Colonel McComsky Plaza. Berth's Garage
Is on the corner facing west, and there,   5
Most days, you'll find Flick Webb, who helps Berth out.

Flick stands tall among the idiot pumps —
Five on a side, the old bubble-head style,

Their rubber elbows hanging loose and low.
One's nostrils are two S's, and his eyes   10
An E and O. And one is squat, without
A head at all—more of a football type.

Once, Flick played for the high school team, the Wizards.
He was good: in fact, the best. In '46,
He bucketed three hundred ninety points,   15
A county record still. The ball loved Flick.
I saw him rack up thirty-eight or forty
In one home game. His hands were like wild birds.

He never learned a trade; he just sells gas,
Checks oil, and changes flats. Once in a while,   20
As a gag, he dribbles an inner tube,
But most of us remember anyway.
His hands are fine and nervous on the lug wrench.
It makes no difference to the lug wrench, though.

Off work, he hangs around Mae's Luncheonette.   25
Grease-grey and kind of coiled, he plays pinball,
Sips lemon cokes, and smokes those thin cigars;
Flick seldom speaks to Mae, just sits and nods
Beyond her face towards the bright applauding tiers
Of Necco Wafers, Nibs, and Juju Beads.   30

A SECOND LOOK

1. Updike shows much about Flick's life by setting up comparisons. How does the description of Pearl Avenue apply to Flick? What is suggested by the description of the pumps?

2. What lines of the poem reveal Flick's talent?

3. What lines show that he lives mainly in the past?

IDEAS FOR WRITING

1. Without using Updike's exact words, describe Flick Webb in a paragraph.

2. Have you known someone like Flick Webb, someone who lives on past glory achieved in any field? Describe this person. Tell your readers (who do not know your subject) what kind of success this individual had and what kind of person he or she is now.

COMES THE REVOLUTION

Time

LOOKING FORWARD

The "revolution" in the title refers to the increase in the number of women in sports. The specific examples at the beginning indicate the many types of sports in which women now participate. But, as the article also points out, this is part of a larger change. More and more people are now enjoying sports, regardless of talent, age, or sex.

HELP WITH WORDS

intensity *(paragraph 1):* strong feeling

charges *(paragraph 1):* those for whom one is responsible

incubator *(paragraph 2):* a machine to aid in the growth of infants or young animals

fanatical *(paragraph 2):* extremely enthusiastic

defiant *(paragraph 2):* rebellious

kaleidoscope *(paragraph 3):* a tube that shows changing patterns of many colors and shapes

buttressed *(paragraph 6):* supported

mandates *(paragraph 6):* orders

stigma *(paragraph 6):* a sign of disgrace

vigor *(paragraph 7):* strength, energy

tenacity *(paragraph 7):* staying power

unseemly *(paragraph 11):* improper

misnomer *(paragraph 11):* wrong name

---

1   **S**teve Sweeney paces the sideline, shoulders hunched against the elements. A steady downpour has turned an Atlanta soccer field into a grassy bog. A few yards away, his team of eight- and nine-year-olds, sporting regulation shirts and shorts, churns after the skittering ball. One minute, all is professional intensity as the players struggle to start a play. The next, there is childhood glee in splashing through a huge puddle that has formed in front of one goal. Sweeney squints at his charges and shouts, "Girls, you gotta pass! Come on, Heather!"

2   At eight, Kim Edwards is in the incubator of the national pastime—tee-ball. There are no pitchers in the pre-Little League league. The ball is placed on a waist-high, adjustable tee, and for five innings the kids whack away. Kim is one of the hottest tee-ball players in Dayton and a fanatical follower of the Cincinnati Reds. Her position is second base. She pulls a Reds cap down over her hair, punches her glove, drops her red-jacketed arms down to rest on red pants, and waits for the action. Kim has but a single ambition: to play for her beloved Reds. When a male onlooker points out that no woman has ever played big league baseball, Kim's face, a mass of strawberry freckles, is a study in defiant dismissal: "So?"

3   The raw wind of a late-spring chill bites through Philadelphia's Franklin Field, but it cannot dull the excitement of the moment. For the first time in the eighty-four year history of the Penn Relays, the world's largest and oldest meet of its kind, an afternoon of women's track and field competition is scheduled. The infield shimmers with color, a kaleidoscope of uniforms and warmup suits. One thousand college and high school athletes jog slowly back and forth, stretch and massage tight muscles, crouch in imaginary starting blocks, huddle with coaches for last-minute strategy sessions, or loll on the synthetic green turf, sipping cocoa and waiting. Susan White, a nineteen-year-old hurdler from the University of Maryland, surveys the scene. There is a trace of awe

in her voice: "When I was in high school, I never dreamed of competing in a national meet. People are finally accepting us as athletes."

4   Golfer Carol Mann is chatting with friends outside the clubhouse when a twelve-year-old girl walks up, politely clears her throat and asks for an autograph. Mann bends down—it's a long way from six-foot, three-inch Mann to fan—and talks softly as she writes. After several moments, the girl returns, wide-eyed, to waiting parents. Mann straightens and smiles. "Five years ago, little girls never walked up to tell me they wanted to be a professional golfer. Now it happens all the time. Things are changing, things are changing."

5   They are indeed. On athletic fields and playgrounds and in parks and gymnasiums across the country, a new player has joined the grand game that is sporting competition, and she's a girl. As the long summer begins, not only is she learning to hit a two-fisted backhand like Chris Evert's and turn a back flip like Olga Korbut's, she is also learning to jam a hitter with a fast ball. Season by season, whether aged six, sixty, or beyond, she is running, jumping, hitting, and throwing as U.S. women have never done before. She is trying everything from jogging to ice hockey, lacrosse and rugby, and in the process acquiring a new sense of self, and of self-confidence in her physical abilities and her potential. She is leading a revolution that is one of the most exciting and one of the most important in the history of sport. Says Joan Warrington, executive secretary of the Association for Intercollegiate Athletics for Women: "Women no longer feel that taking part in athletics is a privilege. They believe it is a right."

6   Spurred by the fitness craze, fired up by the feminist movement and buttressed by court rulings and legislative mandates, women have been moving from miniskirted cheerleading on the sidelines for the boys to playing, and playing hard, for themselves. Says Liz Murphy, coordinator of women's athletics at the University of Georgia: "The stigma is nearly erased. Sweating girls are becoming socially acceptable." . . .

7   If, as folklore and public have long insisted, sport is good for people, if it builds a better society by encouraging mental and physical vigor, courage and tenacity, then the revolution in women's sports holds a bright promise for the future. One city in which the future is now is Cedar Rapids, Iowa. In 1969, well before law, much less custom, required the city to make any

reforms, Cedar Rapids opened its public school athletic program to girls and, equally important, to the less gifted boys traditionally squeezed out by win-oriented athletic systems. Says Tom Ecker, head of school athletics, "Our program exists to develop good kids, not to serve as a training ground for the universities and pros."

8   Some seven thousand students, nearly three thousand of them girls, compete on teams with a firm no-cut policy. Everyone gets a chance to play. Teams are fielded according to skill levels, and a struggle between junior varsity and C-squad basketball teams is as enthusiastically contested as a varsity clash. Cedar Rapids' schoolgirl athletes compete in nine sports, guided by 144 coaches. Access to training equipment is equal too. The result has been unparalleled athletic success. In the past eight years, Cedar Rapids' boys and girls teams have finished among the state's top three sixty-eight times, winning thirty team championships in ten different sports.

9   Girls' athletics have become an accustomed part of the way of life in Cedar Rapids. At a recent girls' track meet, runners, shotputters, hurdlers, high jumpers pitted themselves, one by one, in the age-old contests to run faster, leap higher, throw farther. For many, there were accomplishments they once would have thought impossible. A mile relay team fell into triumphant embrace when word came of qualification for the state finals. Team members shouted the joy of victory—"We did it!"—and then asked permission to break training: "Now can we go to the Dairy Queen, Coach?" Granted.

10   The mile run was won by seventeen-year-old Julie Nolan of Jefferson High School. Sport is, and will remain, part of her life. "I've been running since the fifth or sixth grade. I want to run in college and then run in marathons." She admires Marathoner Miki Gorman, who ran her fastest when she was in her forties. "That's what I'd like to be doing," she says. Asked if she has been treated differently since she got involved in sports, this once-and-future athlete seemed perplexed: "I don't know, because I've always been an athlete."

11   Kelly Galliher, fifteen, has grown up in the Cedar Rapids system that celebrates sport for all. The attitudes and resistance that have stunted women's athleticism elsewhere are foreign to Kelly, a sprinter. Does she know that sports are, in some quarters, still viewed as unseemly for young women? "That's ridiculous.

Boys sweat, and we're going to sweat. We call it getting out and trying." She has no memories of disapproval from parents or peers. And she has never been called the terrible misnomer that long and unfairly condemned athletic girls. "Tomboy? That idea has gone out here." It's vanishing everywhere.

A SECOND LOOK

1. Look carefully at the first four paragraphs. Why are the examples placed in the order they are?

2. Look at the details in these paragraphs. How does the writer make each example seem attractive and special?

3. What is special about the sports program in Cedar Rapids?

4. This article was written in 1978. Has the revolution now moved forward or slowed down?

IDEAS FOR WRITING

1. Many public school systems and colleges are faced with shrinking funds for athletics. Should the available money be divided so that a number of sports programs receive support, or should the funds be concentrated in those major programs that are already proven successes? Write a paper in which you take one side of this question or the other. Use as many facts as you can to strengthen your case.

2. In a section of this article not printed here, the author says that through athletic competition children learn lessons about success and failure that will help them later in life. Tell about an experience in which you or someone you know learned such a lesson.

FOUL SHOT

Edwin A. Hoey

LOOKING FORWARD

This short poem describes the final two seconds of a basketball game, when a young player puts up the winning shot. Pay special attention to the verbs that bring the action to life.

HELP WITH WORDS

exasperates *(line 24):* uses up one's patience

plays it coy *(line 25):* pretends to hold back

With two 60's stuck on the scoreboard
And two seconds hanging on the clock,
The solemn boy in the center of eyes,
Squeezed by silence,
Seeks out the line with his feet,   5
Soothes his hands along his uniform,
Gently drums the ball against the floor,
Then measures the waiting net,
Raises the ball on his right hand,
Balances it with his left,   10
Calms it with fingertips,
Breathes,
Crouches,
Waits,

And then through a stretching of stillness,   15
Nudges it upward.

The ball
Slides up and out,
Lands,
Leans,   20
Wobbles,
Wavers,
Hesitates,
Exasperates,
Plays it coy,   25
Until every face begs with unsounding screams—
And then
        And then
                And then,
Right before ROAR-UP,
Dives down and through.   30

A SECOND LOOK

1. List the words in the poem that add to the feeling of tension.

2. Soothes (line 6), drums (line 7), and calms (line 11) are not the words you would expect. What words would you usually expect here? Why does the author use the unusual?

MAKING CONNECTIONS

1. Although Flick Webb is not black, he seems to be the sort of victim of sports that Arthur Ashe is describing in his letter. Is it possible to extend Ashe's warnings to others involved in sports? What types of players are at risk?

2. If, as Arthur Ashe and John Updike suggest, athletics can distract young people from their schoolwork and give them false values and ideas about success, why is the growing participation of girls in sports presented as a positive development in the *Time* article?

FEARS

YES, YOU CAN FACE UP TO YOUR FEARS

Lois B. Morris

LOOKING FORWARD

Lois B. Morris is a free-lance author who often writes about health and human behavior. In this article, she describes the kinds of fears that cause anxiety and prevent otherwise capable people from accomplishing their goals. Morris also explains how experts say these fears can be overcome.

HELP WITH WORDS

phobia *(paragraph 4):* an unreasonable fear that occurs repeatedly

subside *(paragraph 7):* become less active

confront *(paragraph 8):* face up to

immobilizes *(paragraph 10):* stops movement

harbor *(paragraph 12):* to hold in the mind

reluctance *(paragraph 12):* unwillingness

unacknowledged *(paragraph 12):* unadmitted

emerged *(paragraph 14):* came into view

symbolically *(paragraph 14):* standing for something else

asserting *(paragraph 14):* putting forward with confidence

therapeutic *(paragraph 16):* that which treats or cures a disease

podium *(paragraph 19):* speaker's stand

desensitized *(paragraph 20):* lessened the reaction to

vibrant *(paragraph 20):* lively

venture *(paragraph 23):* dare to go

---

1   "I thought I was going to die," Christie Rhodes says. "I felt cold and clammy, and couldn't seem to draw a breath. I was clutching the side of the boat and my hands felt suddenly numb."

2   Everybody's afraid of something. Christie's . . . deepest fear was being out on the water. Yet there she was, sailing on Lake Michigan on her first date with Paul Fried, trying to hide her panic.

3   Christie is a bold and adventurous woman, a super-risk-taker. She's confident and accomplished and no one realizes she has fears like anybody else. No one knew how, after she gave up teaching high school to go to medical school, she had to struggle against her fear of competing in a "man's field."

4   Our fears can cripple us in many ways, especially if they're an excuse to protect ourselves against taking risks, says psychiatrist Arthur B. Hardy, M.D., of Menlo Park, California. He's the founder of a phobia treatment program called TERRAP—short for territorial apprehensiveness—which is now offered at forty-seven centers around the country. . . .

5   Christie's fear of the water began at age four, when a rowboat she and her uncle were in capsized. Though her uncle grabbed on to her immediately and she was never in danger, the dread remained. Christie consistently avoided boating until that day, twenty-three years later, when Paul invited her to go sailing.

6   "Even thinking about it panicked me," she recalls. "I was all ready to suggest tennis instead, when suddenly I got angry at myself. If I wanted to go sailing with this man, why couldn't I? I hate it when something gets in my way, and here I was allowing a silly fear to stop me."

FOOTHILL COLLEGE BOOKSTORE

(415) 960.4305 (415) 944 -7305

```
1   25  1
      09    EM
      05    EM
            19.44 TX  E
            1.3 6 TX
            20.80  TL
            20.80 CA
      02  3847
```

SELL BACK POLICY

SELL YOUR NEW & USED BOOKS FOR CASH AT THE BOOKSTORE DURING FINALS WEEK. YOUR BOOKS MAY BE WORTH UP TO 50% — — RECEIPTS NOT NEEDED —

THE BOOKSTORE CANNOT GUARANTEE THE BUYBACK OF ANY BOOK AT ANYTIME.

7   It wasn't easy. Although she sensed that if she could endure her terror long enough the feeling would begin to subside, it was a full year before she was truly comfortable on a boat. Now, four years later, Christie Rhodes, M.D., can't think of any activity she's more fond of than sailing with Paul, who's now her husband.

8   The technique that Christie used to overcome her fear is called "flooding" by psychotherapists who specialize in the treatment of phobias and fears. It is the quickest, but most difficult, method. "You jump in, confront the discomfort without any excuses and without trying to build up to it," says psychologist William Golden. . . . "You say to yourself, 'This is what I want to achieve and I'm going to go through it. I know it's going to feel uncomfortable, but it's worth it.'"

9   Determining whether it is worth it is the first step. Are all fears really worth eliminating?

10   Dr. Hardy and most mental health professionals believe that a fear is worth confronting if it immobilizes, restricts or otherwise prevents you from leading a full, active life and you're making personal and professional sacrifices to avoid it. It is not worth confronting if you use the fear to benefit your life. Dr. Golden calls the latter kind of avoidance "adaptive." The very common fear of public speaking, for example, is adaptive if it leads you to rehearse and master your material. It is maladaptive if it causes you to turn down speaking engagements that could advance your career.

11   Usually, the awful discomfort linked to a fear of a particular situation or thing (such as fear of driving, taking a test, sexual aggression, or heights) disappears when we simply avoid the action or remove ourselves from the threat: No plane ride, no fear of flying. But then the avoidance itself becomes a problem—and often a crippling one.

12   "There are two kinds of avoidance," explains Dr. Golden. "One is habitual and complete, as with phobias. The other is procrastination—putting things off." Thus, if you delay paying bills or writing reports or answering letters, you may harbor fears you're refusing to admit you have. Also, the avoidance of intimate relationships, a reluctance to leave an unfulfilling job or to ask for a raise, the refusal to invest money, and even insomnia are often signs of unacknowledged fears, says Samuel V. Dunkell, M.D., assistant clinical professor of psychiatry at New York Hospital/Cornell Medical Center.

13 Julia Bernstein, for example, is in her forties and an outspoken activist for women's causes. She has always loved politics but was so afraid of public speaking that, while in her twenties, she decided against a political career and went into merchandising instead. "I would tell myself that I wasn't strong enough or smart enough to be in politics," she explains today. "And after I married, every time I was tempted to hop onto somebody's bandwagon, I'd tell myself that my husband wouldn't like it." Yet it was he who suggested that Julia run for a seat on the local board of education.

14 Julia agreed—and quickly found herself suffering from constant anxiety. She consulted a therapist. The reasons behind her fear soon emerged. "In my case, it had to do with my fear of competing with my older sister," she says. "Symbolically, public speaking meant standing up and speaking for myself, asserting my own identity—and that was a terrible conflict for me."

15 To chart the extent of your fears, Dr. Golden recommends that you make a list of the things that frighten you. You are probably already aware of any phobias you may have, since such intense fears are marked by panic attacks and alarm reactions. But inhale deeply and be very frank with yourself. You'll soon be able to understand the damage you may be doing by giving in to your fears if you measure your list against your personal and professional goals—both short- and long-term. Then ask yourself: What should I be doing that I'm not doing now? If you have a fear of flying, and yet you want to be manager for Midwest division sales in five years, you'd better start dealing with this obstacle to your advancement now. If you enjoy swimming, but even in a pool you worry about shark attacks, the price for not standing up to that fear will depend on your priorities. Just how important is swimming to you? . . .

16 While therapeutic approaches to fear vary, most therapists agree that there is no way around doing exactly what you fear or exposing yourself to it—if you can find a way around it, you probably don't need a treatment program. Like the fallen rider who climbs back on her horse, the quicker you can get it over with, says Dr. Hardy, the less likely your fear will take root and spread.

17 Dealing with fear really means coping with anxiety. In her book *Women and Anxiety*, psychiatrist Helen A. De Rosis, M.D., writes, "Anxiety is a feeling of dread, a nameless fear that distracts the minds and hearts of people of all ages." But, she also

says, "Most bouts of anxiety are manageable, as well as self-limited." No matter how bad it is, anxiety always passes—and that's the key to toughing out your fears.

18   "Any new venture should have some anxiety," says Dr. Hardy. "It's unfamiliar territory and you don't have your confidence up yet. Once you do, your anxiety decreases." If you can endure a feared situation long enough to gain some confidence—as in giving a speech, performing before an audience, writing a company memo or asking an important favor—the self-assurance itself becomes convincing.

19   Once you have that confidence, you can choose the method of confronting your fear that's best suited to you. Christie Rhodes' sink-or-swim sailing technique was her way of coping. Julia Bernstein, the future politician, needed a more gradual approach to accustom herself to stepping up to a podium.

20   At her therapist's suggestion, Julia first practiced speaking into a tape recorder, then into a mirror. Next, she delivered the speech before her husband, and another time, in front of his parents and their neighbors. By pushing herself further and further into her fear, Julia "desensitized" it. It was a difficult process, requiring serious motivation. Today she's still a little nervous before giving a speech, but feels it's almost a kind of energy she can harness for a good, vibrant delivery. More and more she even enjoys herself. . . .

21   If, by using either approach, you still can't face your fears, you may have to dig deeper and move to traditional psychotherapy. . . .

22   Maybe the only thing you'll need, however, is a change in attitude, something that experts call a "counterphobic" attitude—the desire to stand up, even if shaking and quaking, to what we fear. "Everybody's frightened. Everybody's anxious. Everybody's worried. In fact the people who seem least so, like heroes, are often more frightened than anyone else," says New York psychoanalyst Lee Minoff. "The soldier might have so great a fear of dying that the only way he can deal with it is to rush right into combat in a counterphobic way. And he becomes the hero." . . .

23   "People who are successful venture much farther out on a limb," Dr. Dunkell says. "They usually are rewarded eventually, if only because by enduring their fear and going on despite the discomfort, they allow a wider range of opportunities into their lives."

24   There are other, unexpected payoffs as well. More than one fear may topple [when we attack] only one. In the same way that unconfronted fears mushroom, says Dr. Golden, success also multiplies—he calls it the "ripple effect."

25   Secondly, being able to do something you've long avoided causes a lifelong "high." Says Dr. Dunkell, "Once the fear is overcome, people take an exaggerated pleasure in their former terror. My wife used to have a little phobia about flying. Now while to most people flying is a perhaps tedious necessity of modern life, for her each time is a real adventure."

26   Write those reports and get up on that stage and set sail in that boat and love it?

27   Go ahead and try. You have nothing to fear.

A SECOND LOOK

1. In addition to explaining and giving examples of phobias, Morris also describes a process the reader can follow to overcome his or her own phobias. Find the steps in this process, beginning in paragraph 9.

2. Morris obviously has consulted a number of outside sources to collect the material for her article. What advantages are gained from using these sources? Check a paragraph in which a source appears (perhaps paragraph 4, 12, or 17). How does Morris give credit for the information that she borrows from someone else?

3. In paragraph 10 two technical terms, *adaptive* and *maladaptive*, are defined. Examine the definitions. What does the author do to make the terms clear to the reader?

4. One technique for overcoming a phobia is called "flooding." Describe this cure. What alternative method is suggested?

5. The article mentions several advantages of overcoming a phobia. What are they?

IDEAS FOR WRITING

Try to think of something that you know how to do but that others might not know as much about. Your topic can come from any category—how to rappel, how to raise money for charity, how to get through a lonely weekend, how to budget your income, and so on. Then make a numbered list of the steps necessary to complete the project. Check the list carefully to be sure that no step is left out and that the steps are listed in the right order.

Your first paragraph should introduce the topic and catch the reader's interest. The body of the paper should present the steps necessary to complete the process. These should be explained very clearly. Imagine the reader following your directions. Are there any points at which a person unfamiliar with the process might be confused? Do any words need to be defined?

If you need to use an outside source to add to your knowledge of the topic, remember to mention the name of the expert and to give credit for the information.

LEARNING TO LIVE WITH THE BOMB

Phyllis La Farge

LOOKING FORWARD

In this essay, Phyllis La Farge analyzes some of the reasons that young people, especially between the ages of twelve and fourteen, develop an intense fear of nuclear war. Her essay reports a part of her research on the topic of nuclear fear which is the subject of her recent book, *The Strangelove Legacy*.

HELP WITH WORDS

intractable *(paragraph 1):* difficult to manage

cognitive development *(paragraph 2):* the process by which reasoning ability is developed

decimate *(paragraph 6):* destroy

deter *(paragraph 7):* prevent

agenda *(paragraph 12):* a list of things to be done

explicit *(paragraph 12):* specific and detailed

apocalyptic awareness *(paragraph 25):* awareness of future disaster

relegated *(paragraph 30):* sent away to

fervently *(paragraph 32):* with strong emotion

1   **M**ost researchers studying the attitudes of young people towards a variety of public issues have found that young adolescents from twelve to fourteen years of age are more apt to be concerned intensely about the threat of nuclear war than younger children or older adolescents. It is easy to imagine that they are more afraid than younger children because they know more—about nuclear weapons, about the intractable nature of international politics, about the nature of war. Greater knowledge leads to an intensified emotional response. But why are young adolescents more afraid than older adolescents?

2   The cognitive development that takes place during adolescence offers one answer. One of the key changes of adolescence is the development of a capacity to think more abstractly, including the ability to think about one's thoughts. This capacity enables the adult, in the words of the renowned psychologist Sibylle Escalona, to "schematize the way you look at things," that is, to fit perceptions and experience into a highly developed intellectual framework. In such a framework, Escalona noted to me, "you don't see a new fact so clearly. It becomes enmeshed and embedded in the scheme." This step in intellectual development begins in preadolescence or early adolescence, but it does not develop all at once or at the same rate in every individual and may not be fully evident until the later adolescent years. I believe that the fact that it is not fully accomplished in early adolescence contributes to the young teenager's greater fear of nuclear war. He cannot schematize the way he looks at things and therefore distance himself from their impact.

3   A fourteen-year-old, Russ, wrote:

4   The idea of nuclear war scares me. I'm only fourteen years old and I have no wish to die or even to be a survivor in a postnuclear world. I have my whole life ahead of me, and I don't want my world to be turned upside down.

5   I can find only one good thing about the effects of preparing for war. When the Russians build newer and better weapons we have to develop newer and better weapons to counteract theirs. This is causing a fast increase in all technology, giving us better stuff until, of course, war happens.

6   Another thing I don't understand is the nuclear freeze. If we freeze our weaponry and the U.S.S.R. freezes its weaponry, some other country will build lots of bombs and decimate our countries.

7   I feel that we have way too many weapons. We could start

dismantling warheads at the same time as Russia. We could then only keep enough to deter attacks and sign treaties with many other countries, stopping the advance of nuclear technology.

8 Compared with the letters and essays of . . . fourth graders . . . , Russ's essay represents a big step toward maturity in the range of topics tackled, grasp of issues or problems, and in the writer's ability to express himself.

9 A young adolescent like Russ has acquired a considerable knowledge of the world, and this knowledge may, in the case of some young people, include information about the nature of nuclear weapons, their delivery systems, and the arms race in general. But he may not yet be able to cushion or distance himself with the kind of abstract thinking used by older adolescents and adults. In the words of psychiatrist John Mack, young adolescents have "a kind of raw vision" of the danger and consequences of nuclear war.

10 Furthermore, their still limited knowledge of social and political institutions may restrict their understanding of the way in which people can work together to prevent conflict and of the way in which the individual leader, at least in a democratic society, is restrained by social and political institutions and their representatives.

11 Another answer to questions concerning adolescents' anxiety about nuclear war can be found in the importance they attach to the future.

12 With their maturing bodies, their discovery of sexuality, their new self-consciousness, and their concern with self-definition apart from family, adolescents make the future their agenda in a way that is more explicit and impatient than is true for younger children. I believe that the fact that younger adolescents feel "further" from that future than older adolescents and far more untested and unsure in relation to what it promises aggravates their concern that it will be taken away from them.

13 One young adolescent wrote:

14 There isn't a middle to my life yet, so how can there be an end? I want to have lots of babies and become a grandmother and an actor.

15 At the same time, both older and younger adolescents need the future, as people of all ages do, to underwrite intention, purpose,

and commitment, to give weight to the reality of the present; but they need it more than an adult because their goals and commitments—and their sense of who they are—are not supported by habit or achievement to the same degree as an adult. One adolescent struggled with these big issues:

16 I'm angry because I feel I won't have a future like most people and I ask myself why do I take classes I hate, such as science and math when maybe I won't live to use my knowledge from those classes in college. I feel helpless. I keep trying to kid myself and forget about any possibilities of a nuclear war.

17 In another time and culture, adolescents might already be mothers or fathers and have started on their life's work, but today in our society they must wait, especially if they want to "get ahead," and this makes confidence in the future vital to their sense of purpose.

18 If an adolescent lets in the nuclear vision in a deep and vivid way, he or she is confronted with death anxiety, a sense of meaninglessness and helplessness, a feeling that life is out of control—and often rage at the possibility of being cheated of a chance at adult life.

19 Intense awareness may be triggered by many factors—a personal confrontation with death, which lowers defenses against thinking of the nuclear issue, or something that makes the power of the weapons concrete, such as photos or a film. For one young man I spoke with, it was a photo of a watch that stopped at the time of Hiroshima.

20 A high school sophomore described this process:

21 Ever since I have been aware of world matters, I have known about nuclear weapons. I was never really scared of the thought of nuclear war before; I think that is because I never really knew what nuclear war would mean.

22 Just in the past year I learned what a nuclear reaction was. Then I started becoming more and more aware of how much damage nuclear weapons could do.

23 A young antinuclear activist echoed these words. "I think I was aware of the issue for a long time because my older sister was interested. I can remember having talks with her about it back to fourth grade. But I was like the rest of the public, I hid behind my

little shield. I wanted to know my few facts, but I didn't want to know more."

24   When the "little shield" is pierced or dropped, awareness can be intense and painful. For a few the subject becomes all absorbing. "I came to the point where I couldn't just not think about it," one teenager said. Many who become aware feel confused, as if the ordinary framework of reality were all at once called into question.

25   Apocalyptic awareness and feelings of helplessness and being out of control are not tolerable for more than a brief period. Confronted by them, a young person has two choices. He can choose activism—a choice made by a small number of teenagers in the last several years—which will help him maintain some degree of awareness without being engulfed or paralyzed by it. Or after a period of intense awareness, he can mend the "little shield" and in one way or another "manage" awareness.

26   Awareness does not disappear entirely even while it is being "managed." Many describe it as going "in and out" of their consciousness:

27   I don't want to think about a nuclear war because it scares me. I try to put it out of my mind, but it comes up over and over again.

28   Another teenager wrote:

29   Sometimes, I get some of these feelings to express my concern. But also at other times it makes me feel better to keep these feelings inside. . . . I would rather live my life in joy than live it in constant fear.

30   For some, awareness is relegated to the world of dream and nightmare:

31   I have had nightmares with the alert coming over the television and hordes of blackened people screaming to the sky. But the dreams of children do nothing positive. We must join together to change the present situation. We must have both attainable and ideal goals. We must never lose hope.

32   Never losing hope is what all parents fervently want for their children, but when it comes to complex public issues, different parents pursue different approaches. Those who are themselves

political activists teach their children that "joining together" and working for a cause one cares about is the best way to feel hopeful, whatever the cause and whatever their political stripe. Those who are sustained by religious faith teach their children that faith is the biggest source of hope. In recent years this approach includes those whose religious beliefs teach them that the world will soon end in global conflict, but the faithful will be spared.

33   The great majority of parents, however, try to encourage hopefulness by keeping silent about the nuclear weapons, the arms race, and other issues, such as adequate disposal of radioactive and chemical wastes, that may be of concern to children. The difficulty with this approach is that in an era of television there is no way of protecting children once they are of school age from at least some exposure to a public issue—and often the child's awareness may be far greater than a parent suspects.

34   In our times, I believe that true protection must take a different form than silence: raising children who will be able and willing to think about complex issues, make judgments about the policies of their leaders, and act or vote on the basis of their judgments. Parents don't have to become experts to encourage such capacities, although the more information about public issues they bring into the home, the better. The foundations of a sense of empowerment or competence with respect to "big-world" issues can be fostered by giving children a sense that no subject is taboo; that any question they have can and will be answered (although sometimes the answer will be complex); that they have a duty to play a responsible role first in their home and later in their community and are competent to do so.

35   Moreover, parents need not feel that it falls to them alone to build such competence. They can press their children's schools to provide good current-events education in the upper grades, to train children in thinking critically about issues, and to provide opportunities for responsibility within the community of the school itself.

A SECOND LOOK

1. To answer the question she asks at the end of paragraph 1, La Farge analyzes cases and gives reasons. These reasons are given in paragraphs 2, 10, and 11. State each one clearly.

2. One device La Farge uses to make her writing vivid is quotations from letters written by young people about nuclear war. How does the fourteen-year-old Russ cope with his fears of nuclear war?

3. In paragraph 23, a young person described as an anti-nuclear activist says she hid behind her "little shield." To what does she refer?

4. Once a young person experiences an intense awareness of the dangers of nuclear war, he or she has, according to La Farge, two choices. What are they?

5. La Farge explains that parents try to help their children by teaching them religious beliefs or by protecting them from information about nuclear war. She, however, advises another way of helping. What is it?

IDEAS FOR WRITING

La Farge quotes from a number of letters which adolescents wrote to express their feelings about the nuclear threat. What are your own feelings? Have you thought about the possibility of nuclear war? If so, how have you coped with such fears? In a letter, try expressing your own feelings about the nuclear threat. You may wish to address your letter to a national leader, to your parents, to your peers, or perhaps to your children. Try to make the letter fit the audience you choose.

TEN MINUTES OF HORROR

Ed Magnuson

LOOKING FORWARD

Ed Magnuson's account of the attacks on passengers at Rome and Vienna airports focuses on one major source of fear in this decade: terrorism. The report emphasizes the horror of unsuspecting, innocent people being wounded and killed, and the lingering fear that this violence will be repeated.

HELP WITH WORDS

laden *(paragraph 1):* loaded

attaché *(paragraph 2):* a military officer attached to an embassy

frenzy *(paragraph 2):* wild excitement

carnage *(paragraph 2):* slaughter

commandeered *(paragraph 5):* seized

vulnerability *(paragraph 6):* openness to attack or harm

emanates *(paragraph 6):* flows from

fragility *(paragraph 6):* breakableness, delicacy

dissident *(paragraph 6):* disagreeing in attitude or opinion

retaliation *(paragraph 6):* an action taken to get even or strike back

inevitable *(paragraph 12):* certain, unavoidable

---

1   **L**ong lines of holiday travelers pushing heavily laden baggage carts were waiting in the main departure lounge of Rome's Leonardo da Vinci Airport. Hardly anyone paid

much attention to four dark-complexioned young men who mingled with the crowd. One wore an expensive gray suit and camel's hair topcoat. Two were in blue jeans and jackets, and had pulled scarves partly over their faces. The fourth sported a green beret. They were not traveling light: they carried 13 hand grenades and four AK-47 automatic rifles.

2   At 9:03 A.M., one of the men threw a grenade toward a nearby espresso bar and hamburger counter, where General Donato Miranda Acosta, the military attaché at the Mexican embassy in Rome, was sipping coffee with his secretary, Genoveva Jaime Cisneros, who was there to see him and his family off on a vacation trip to Frankfurt. Miranda Acosta and Cisneros were probably the first to be killed. Then the attackers raked the 820-foot-long terminal with bullets, hitting people waiting for an El Al flight and others at nearby TWA and Pan Am counters. The men jumped up and down in a frenzy, screaming as they fired, and security guards shot back. "People were falling all over the place," recalled Anna Girometta, who operates a gift shop near the coffee bar. "It seemed to go on forever." Five minutes later, the carnage was over. The toll: 15 people dead, including three of the terrorists, and 74 wounded.

3   At about the time that the shooting stopped at Leonardo da Vinci, three men in dirty pants and combat jackets ran up the steps to the second-floor departure area at Vienna's Schwechat Airport. They opened fire with AK-47s. Passengers waiting to check in for El Al Flight 364 to Tel Aviv threw themselves on the floor or leaped over ticket counters in panic. Police and El Al security guards returned the fire, but the terrorists managed to get within 30 feet of the counter. They rolled three hand grenades across the floor like bowling balls toward their victims.

4   Eckehard Kaerner, 50, an Austrian high school teacher headed for some vacation study in Israel, died of multiple wounds under a brightly lit Christmas tree near the El Al counter. "Suddenly there was this terrible noise, not single shots but real explosions," said a Viennese man who jumped behind a counter. "Three or four meters to my left, three people had fallen to the ground. There was a small child, all bloodied, its mother who was also wounded, and a man who lay bleeding and seemed dead. To my right another man had fallen and did not budge anymore."

5   Within two minutes after the shooting began, the gunmen

escaped down a flight of stairs and headed for an employee garage, where one of them pulled a knife on an airport official and commandeered his Mercedes-Benz. In a running gun battle with police, the terrorists tossed a grenade at a pursuing patrol car (it missed), and police bullets flattened a tire and pierced the gas tank of the Mercedes. Just two miles from the airport, the killers were stopped. The toll: three dead, including one of the terrorists, and 47 wounded.

6   In just ten terror-filled minutes last Friday, the civilized world was thus given yet another reminder of its vulnerability at the hands of suicidal terrorists, of the lethal instability that emanates from the Middle East and finally, of life's terrifying fragility. Responsibility for the attacks was claimed by a dissident Palestine Liberation Organization splinter group. The assaults touched off widespread debate about possible motives, about the likelihood of Israeli retaliation, and about whether the massacres could have been prevented in the first place.

7   Interpol, the Paris-based anticrime organization, had warned early in December that terrorists, "probably of Arab origin," might strike an airport during the Christmas holidays. Officials in a few West European countries had already taken precautions. At Rome's airport, a balcony overlooking the ticket counters had been closed. Both the Charles de Gaulle and Orly airports outside Paris were being watched by extra squads of national police. Undercover detectives drifted among the crowds near check-in counters at London's Heathrow. Every taxiing El Al airliner at major European airports was trailed by armored cars carrying police with machine guns. Screening measures were in effect last week at Rome and Vienna, but to little avail: the massacres occurred well away from the passenger gates.

8   At Leonardo da Vinci, Daniela Simpson was outside the terminal walking the family dog while her husband Victor, the Associated Press news editor in Rome, was checking bags and obtaining boarding passes for the couple and their two children for a TWA flight to New York. "Suddenly there was a shattering noise . . . and two distinct machine-gun bursts," recalled Mrs. Simpson, who reports in Rome as a TIME stringer. "And then silence. I rushed in to screams and cries, and saw my husband dripping blood from his hand and my son on the floor, shot in the stomach. They were O.K., but I lost my daughter." Simpson had

dropped on top of his two children when the firing began. Michael, 9, survived, but Natasha, 11, was dead on arrival at a local hospital. . . .

9 The P.L.O. quickly denied that it had anything to do with last week's airport assaults. Arafat in November denounced terrorist activities outside Israeli-occupied territory. But in Tel Aviv, Defense Minister Yitzhak Rabin claimed that the newest attacks showed that "the Palestinian terrorist organizations are trying to reach us and harm us wherever they can." Israeli Foreign Ministry spokesman Avi Pazner warned that "Israel will continue its struggle against terrorism in every place and at any time that it sees fit."

10 There was little doubt that Israel would strike back. The only real questions were how soon and against what targets. "You bet the Israelis are going to retaliate," observed a top-ranking U.S. intelligence official. "It was an attack aimed against them, and they will not let this go by." . . .

11 The airport terrorism was especially unsettling to Italy and Austria, which have developed relatively good relations with the P.L.O. in recent years. In addition, the tactic of shooting up an airport area that anyone can enter without going through personal and baggage screening troubled officials who supervise airport security. "We can move passenger check-ins further away from airports," said Vienna's Lord Mayor Helmut Zilk. "But we can't keep them secret."

12 Even more worrisome was the possibility that the latest assaults will touch off additional violence. As Michael Simpson, 9, was carried into a Rome hospital last week in a state of near shock, he kept repeating, "It will never end. It will never end." He was, of course, referring to the horrible ordeal he had just endured. But he could just as easily have been describing the inevitable cycle of terror and retaliation that has come to characterize politics in the Middle East.

A SECOND LOOK

1. The first five paragraphs of Magnuson's essay give a detailed account of the two attacks. The author is careful to supply specific details to

help the reader see the people involved as individuals. For example, he writes of one of the terrorists, "One wore an expensive gray suit and camel's hair topcoat." Review paragraphs 1–5 for other examples of detailed description.

2. The main idea of the essay is not made clear until paragraph 6. Restate the idea in your own words. Is it more effective to describe the episodes before stating the generalization?

3. Magnuson uses several quotations in paragraphs 9–11. Why does he quote in these instances? What do the quotations add?

4. Conclusions are sometimes difficult for writers. Magnuson uses a device that often works well: He returns to information presented earlier and reinforces it. Examine paragraph 12 and analyze its content. Then look back at the ends of paragraphs 2 and 8. Does the conclusion adequately restate the main idea?

IDEAS FOR WRITING

In two or three paragraphs, describe some frightening episode you witnessed. Use as many specific details as possible to help the reader visualize the episode and the people involved. Conclude the description with a general statement or statements that point up the main idea to be drawn from the episode. What did it make clear or teach?

HOUSE FEAR

Robert Frost

LOOKING FORWARD

One of America's most famous poets, Robert Frost, shows us in just a few lines what may be the worst kind of fear—the fear of something we do not know and cannot see.

Always—I tell you this they learned—
Always at night when they returned
To the lonely house from far away
To lamps unlighted and fire gone gray,
They learned to rattle the lock and key   5
To give whatever might chance to be
Warning and time to be off in flight:
And preferring the out- to the in-door night,
They learned to leave the house-door wide
Until they had lit the lamp inside.   10

A SECOND LOOK

1. Frost's words are very simple, but he gives us a clear idea of fear. What words help to create this mood?

2. Do you think that what the people fear is real or imagined? Does it matter?

3. Why do the people prefer the outside darkness to the inside darkness?

IDEAS FOR WRITING

Read Frost's poem several times. Become very familiar with it. Then, imagining that you are one of the people in the poem, write one or two paragraphs describing how you feel as you approach the dark house at night. Remember that you are not describing anything physical; you are describing an emotional response. Try to put into words the fear that you feel.

FOGGY FRIDAY

Andrea Smith

LOOKING FORWARD

Andrea Smith describes a frightening experience she and a friend had on a lonely road during a rainy night. Notice how her writing catches and holds the reader's attention.

HELP WITH WORDS

formulate *(paragraph 5):* make, create

dilapidated *(paragraph 7):* decayed, falling apart

veered *(paragraph 9):* turned suddenly

---

1   I have never been more scared in my life. Now when I look back on it, I wonder what we actually saw on that foggy Friday night.

2   It was the night after our last football game of the season. I had asked my best friend Amy to spend the weekend with me because my parents were out of town. We went to the local pizza place where everybody went after a big game. We ordered the usual—a pepperoni pizza and a six-pack of Coke—to go.

3   The drive home took longer than usual because of the dense fog. It was just beginning to rain, and I could barely make out the

road in front of me. Then I saw ahead of us red and yellow flashing lights barely visible through the thick fog, and before long we came upon an accident that was blocking the road. I decided that the best thing to do would be to turn around and go home another way.

4   Now we were driving on a dark, eerie, deserted country road. It began to rain harder, and it was nearly impossible to see. I was talking to Amy and not really paying much attention to the road because I knew it well from driving to and from school almost every day. It was a narrow, winding little road between leafless and seemingly lifeless trees that swayed in the wind. Short bursts of lightning illuminated their naked, skeleton-like forms against the rainy night sky. A little creek flowed quietly beside the crooked road and frogs croaked, adding to the spookiness of the evening.

5   I looked out the windshield, then out the side window, then out the windshield again. My headlights were getting dimmer and dimmer, and I knew what was going to happen. Before I could formulate a plan of action, the engine stopped and I knew that my battery was dead. No one would be driving on this road at such a late hour and there were no houses nearby, so we had no choice. We would have to walk almost two miles to get home.

6   Amy was scared already, and we hadn't even begun our journey. After much persuasion she reluctantly got out of the car, and we began to walk. The farther we walked, the more frightened we became. We were practically clinging to each other in fear.

7   It seemed that we had been walking forever when we finally came to an old landmark that reminded me of a ghost story the older kids used to tell me when I was younger. It was a spring-house nestled among trees on a hillside near the road. The building was old and dilapidated, its bricks crumbling and falling onto the bare ground. The roof was caving in, but still it stood.

8   At the exact moment I opened my mouth to tell Amy my story, she screamed. At first I saw nothing. But there, lurking in the shadows, was the biggest, ugliest, hairiest thing I have ever seen. It started to make its way to the road and we ran. We ran down Polecat Road faster than I ever imagined running in my life. I looked back once and saw it following us on our mad race for my house.

9   We veered off the road into a corn field only partially harvested

and tripped and stumbled over corn stalks. Soon we were in the woods that stand near the edge of the creek. We followed the creek downstream and ran under a bridge. I knew where we were now. Just a little farther. I knew we'd make it.

10   We ran along the edge of the creek, crossed over to the other side, and followed it a few yards more. There we found a path running to the edge of the woods and into my neighbor's back yard. I looked back and saw nothing—but still we ran. We ran until we reached my front door. I searched for my key, found it, put it in the lock and turned. No result. I tried again and it opened. We ran in, locked all the doors and windows, and turned on all the lights. We sat in the living room to watch TV and talk about what had happened.

11   Neither of us knows what she saw that night. Amy thinks it was a bigfoot; I don't know what to think. We sometimes look back at that Friday night and convince ourselves that it was just our imagination, but it's not possible for two people to imagine the same thing at the same time. Is it?

A SECOND LOOK

1. What techniques does Smith use to catch the reader's attention early?

2. Smith does not tell us until paragraph 7 what frightening thing she saw. Why does she wait so long? Should she have let us know earlier?

3. Make a list of adjectives that you think are effective in building up the atmosphere of "spookiness."

4. If this had been your experience and you were describing it, would you have ended the paper differently? If so, how?

IDEAS FOR WRITING

1. Nearly everyone remembers a time when he or she had a frightening experience, something that could be written as a scary story. If you have had such an experience, write an account of it in several para-

graphs. Look again at Smith's essay to see how she creates suspense and holds the reader's attention.

2. Write a paragraph describing a spooky time or place. Concentrate on using effective, perhaps unusual, adjectives. You may wish to use a dictionary of synonyms as you write.

MAKING CONNECTIONS

1. The anxiety caused by the fear of terrorism can be similar to the anxiety that bothers young people when they become aware of the threat of nuclear war. Review the main idea of Magnuson's "Ten Minutes of Terror" (paragraph 6). Discuss whether his description of the fear of terrorism also fits the fear of nuclear attack.

2. Even though Morris describes much less serious and universal topics than La Farge, their suggestions for controlling anxiety are similar. Explain how.

AGING

NEVER TOO OLD: THE ART OF GETTING BETTER

Louise Bernikow

LOOKING FORWARD

Louise Bernikow argues in this essay that American women are victims of unhealthy attitudes toward aging. She uses numerous examples, including personal experiences, as evidence for her argument that women can grow more beautiful and successful as they grow older.

HELP WITH WORDS

fluent *(paragraph 1):* able to speak or write a language easily

eliciting *(paragraph 1):* drawing forth

withered *(paragraph 2):* lost vigor; dried up

compelling *(paragraph 2):* forceful

insidious *(paragraph 3):* more dangerous than appearances would suggest

perpetual *(paragraph 3):* lasting, eternal

idiosyncratic *(paragraph 6):* characteristic of a particular person

constricted *(paragraph 6):* limited, narrow

audacity *(paragraph 7):* daring, boldness

simultaneously *(paragraph 9):* occurring at the same time

impish *(paragraph 9):* like a mischievous child

aura *(paragraph 10):* an atmosphere or quality

autonomous *(paragraph 10):* independent

archive *(paragraph 11):* a collection of documents

mode *(paragraph 14):* a manner of acting

debutante *(paragraph 14):* a girl making an entrance into society

emerge *(paragraph 15):* come into view

---

1   When I was twenty, I was afraid of a lot of things. I worried, for example, about finding myself in bed with Mr. Wonderful at last and looking down, only to discover I had forgotten to shave my legs. Mr. Wonderful would retch and leave. Or I was sure I would translate Dante entirely wrong in Italian class, say something obscene without knowing it, causing snickers from the fluent girls in the back row. I might, I feared, buy the wrong shade of pink cashmere sweater, eliciting similar snickers, now coupled with laughter, from the very same girls, whose perfect color coordination matched their perfect Italian, their perfect dorm rooms and their perfect hold on the universe. These were minor fears. Whatever pits I might fall into, I could always climb out because I was, after all, just twenty, with my whole life ahead of me. But what if I woke up one day to find that I was say, forty?

2   Aging meant sagging—in the face, the body, the spirits. At forty, I thought, a woman was gone, like a skier on a chair lift disappearing over the crest of the mountain. Men might become more powerful, worldly and attractive, but women withered. They inhabited the universe, like the old living room sofa, but nobody paid attention to them. They weren't beautiful, sexy, compelling or exciting. They had no impact. They didn't jump gaily into fountains wearing sequins in the middle of the night or take up calculus or join expeditions to climb the highest mountain in Nepal.

3   I had, in this fear, an insidious cultural disease. Everything around me glorified youthfulness. The popular female stars were perpetual teenagers like Debbie Reynolds, Sandra Dee and Doris Day. Grown-up women existed in some other country, a dull

country. There were "mature" women in ads for tranquilizers. There were "matronly" clothes for the over-forty woman, all grays and browns. There was Eleanor Roosevelt as the model of an older women, striding confidently through the world on half-inch heels. Me, I wanted to play tennis for hours, wear sexy clothes, write at the top of my form. I wanted to keep my zing for years, for decades, forever.

4   Fear of aging is still with us. The disease infects America more than any other country. In Europe, after all, such actresses as Jeanne Moreau, Simone Signoret and Melina Mercouri have remained appealing, exciting women well into what are delicately called their "riper" years. Some of America's current sex symbols, on the other hand, are under twenty-one; some are under seventeen. The market is flooded with products promising a fountain of youth: soaps to make you "fresh-faced," which means young; vitamins to turn your body into a teenager's, no matter how lumpy and sagging it is when you begin wolfing them down. If there is a twenty-year-old today who has masterfully overcome her fear of leg stubble, mistakes in Italian or uncoordinated clothes, but who still catches her breath at the thought of going "over the hill"—passing thirty or even forty—I can't say she's a lunatic. She simply has a bad case of the disease.

5   I'm cured. I got cured by waking up one morning and finding myself over thirty, over forty, not dead, feeling nothing like a sofa. My zing was still in place. I hardly felt that anything had ended. It all seemed to have just started.

6   This has something to do with my own idiosyncratic development and something to do with the cultural conditions under which I managed my arrival at what they used to call middle age. When women of my mother's generation reached forty, most of them had already raised families and were facing "empty nests." The older they got, the less they had to do. Women their age did not return to school or go to work. And because their lives became more constricted as the years passed, they looked and felt older than they actually were. To these women, the idea that life might begin at forty would have seemed crazy. And rightly so.

7   But it's not at all crazy now. Former First Lady Rosalynn Carter gave birth to Amy two months after her fortieth birthday. The number of women having their first child after thirty has more than doubled in the last decade. So has the number of women returning to college. (They do better at their studies,

these doddering older women, than the kids do.) If having babies or hitting the books doesn't seem like the thrill of a lifetime, consider Janet Guthrie, the first and only woman to drive in the Indianapolis 500. (Do sofas drive racing cars?) She was a year shy of forty at the time. Do people over the hill perform with as much vigor or invent with as much audacity and originality as modern dance pioneer Martha Graham did, well past forty? Or paint like Georgia O'Keeffe, sculpt like Louise Nevelson?

8   I look around at my aging friends. The first thing that strikes me is how beautiful they are. I mean physically, although there is a great deal of the spiritual in this beauty. I could trot out a parade of public figures to prove the point—Sophia Loren, Jacqueline Kennedy Onassis, Lauren Bacall, Liv Ullmann, Jane Fonda, Raquel Welch—but I'll stick to the ordinary citizens of my world and to my humble self as a reasonable yardstick.

9   Kitty is sitting there with her legs crossed, red stockings gleaming, something simultaneously impish, excited, authoritative and full of wonder crossing her face as she talks about a project that interests her. Her clothes are wild and original. Her hair is full, flying, electric. Priscilla is standing at the naming ceremony for her newborn daughter, her second child since she turned forty. Her dress is lavender; her eyes brilliant, filled with deep happiness and satisfaction, the kind that comes out of experience rather than innocence.

10   There is experience, too, in Honor's confidence as she dresses to take me out to dinner on my birthday. In a soft black jersey pantsuit, she radiates swagger, elegance, authority; she has the aura of a woman who knows who she is. The younger Honor worried about being fat, bedeviled herself about food, hid, apologized, felt bad. "I feel I'm getting more attractive all the time," she says, brushing her hair. "Standards of beauty are changing. We're beautiful because of our wholeness. I'm so much more autonomous, self-generating. I have a greater sense of the uniqueness of the life I've built and confidence in its ability to sustain me." Clearly, how Honor feels and how she looks are inseparable.

11   This sends me to my personal archive, my photo album. Here, I find the history of my own face as I lay the pictures in a row, like a deck of tarot cards.

12   **1957.** The high school yearbook. The face of innocence and

youth. I look awful. I'm wearing the required black sweater with white lace collar and there is a cheerleader megaphone on a gold chain around my neck. I haven't become anyone yet. I'm quite frantic, and it shows. I'm unhappy and that shows, too.

13   **1960.** The Columbia College Senior Prom. This one makes me cringe. A strand of pearls. Pageboy haircut. Deep-red lipstick. Trying to become what I saw in magazines, imitating grownups. I look as matronly as my mother.

14   **1961.** The college yearbook. The face of someone trying to be someone else. The mode here is obviously debutante. I remember arranging my face to achieve a hollow-cheeked look and worrying about unruly hair—wanting, in every possible way, to be smooth and sophisticated. The following year, I had a nervous breakdown.

15   **1970.** The jacket photograph on my first book. My hair is nearly falling across my face, but still, a face is beginning to emerge. I have some lines around my eyes and some puffiness under them. I had been in love and lived with the man. I had fallen apart and put myself back together. I had a history.

16   **1976.** The face of a woman with confidence. This picture appeared in a book called *Emergence*, by Cynthia MacAdams, which celebrates what the feminist writer, Kate Millett, in the introduction, calls "a new kind of woman." Some of the strength that I like here comes out of a historical context—this is the height of my connection with the Women's Movement—and some comes from being well into my thirties.

17   **1981.** The photograph on the cover of my most recent book, *Among Women*. I am wearing a dress and eye makeup. I am just on the other side of forty and somehow, at last, feel comfortable with all the women I am.

18   I use myself as an example because these personal documents tell what is clearly not a unique story, although it surely goes counter to the cultural mythology that has women growing frumpier and fainter as we age. I feel a great spiritual kinship with Annie Edson Taylor, who celebrated her forty-third birthday by going over Niagara Falls in a barrel. She was the first person and only woman to do so. The year was 1901. I think she'd like being alive today.

A SECOND LOOK

1. Bernikow draws examples from three categories: famous women, personal friends, and her own life. Which category is most convincing? Why?

2. The first paragraph of the essay ends with a question. Is the question ever answered? What effect does Bernikow achieve by using a question here?

3. In paragraph 12 and others that follow, Bernikow uses incomplete sentences. Why? Is this a flaw in her writing? Why or why not?

4. Bernikow calls fear of aging an "insidious cultural disease." Name some of the signs of this disease that she uses as examples in paragraphs 3 and 4. Could you add examples from your own experience?

5. The subtitle of the article is "The Art of Getting Better." According to the author, in what ways do women get better as they age? What accounts for the improvement?

IDEAS FOR WRITING

Choose a person you know well and have known for several years. You should know the person well enough to be acquainted with his or her activities now and in the past. (You could pick your mother or father, a grandparent, or yourself.) Think back to what that person was like five or ten years ago. What did he or she look like, do for a living, have as a hobby, think about most? Then make a list of these characteristics.

Now make a similar list for the person as he or she is now: What does the person now look like, do for a living, and so forth? When you have completed these details, you are ready to write a paper contrasting the person's life now and in the past. Your central point may agree with Bernikow's that older is better, or it may disagree and show that the changes have been for the worse. In either case, state the central idea in the introduction and develop your paper with information from your lists.

UNTIL THE
SINGING STOPS

Don Gold

LOOKING FORWARD

Don Gold interviewed approximately forty men and women over sixty-five as he prepared his book, *Until the Singing Stops*. Although he edited and arranged material from his tape recordings, the words he prints are the actual words of the people being interviewed. Theodore Levy, the speaker in these paragraphs, was in his late eighties when he was interviewed. He is an artist and writer but is best known as a professional magician working under the stage name Theo Doré. When Gold met him, Levy was living in New York (the city where he was born) with Henrietta, his wife of over fifty years.

HELP WITH WORDS

sacrilegious *(paragraph 5):* showing disrespect for something holy

analogy *(paragraph 7):* a comparison

innately *(paragraph 10):* by birth

demeaning *(paragraph 11):* low or undignified

incapacitated *(paragraph 15):* unable to care for oneself

I

1 . . . I was thirty-two before I got married. I was such a good guy, which you don't find today, do you? Well, we finally got engaged and we got married. We had an engagement party that few people have today. We hired a hall, we had a band. And we had a good time. I had tickets for the theater that night. And we left the party and had dinner out. It was beautiful.

2   We had the wedding in a small hall in Harlem. And we stayed overnight at the Majestic Hotel, and we had a trip to Niagara Falls and Canada.

3   We have managed to make it work for fifty-three years. Give and take. There's a thousand jokes about this. A fellow says, "How are you married so long?" He says, "Well, we compromise. When we first got married, my wife wanted red drapes and I wanted green drapes." He said, "So we compromised and got red ones." See? The fellow said to an old man being interviewed, "You're so healthy. You're so vigorous. How do you account for that after more than fifty years of marriage?" He says, "Well, I'll tell you, young fellow. When we first got married, we made an agreement. If we had an argument and my wife was wrong, she had to go into the kitchen, do the dishes, stay there. If we had an argument and I was wrong, I had to leave the house, walk around the block. I've been walking for fifty years."

II

4 Henrietta saved plaid stamps. I don't know how long she saved them up. And then she looked in the book and she said, "I've got four books and a half, what can we get? What do we need?" We need a card table. All right? So we get the books, and we went down to Eighty-first Street and Third Avenue and we gave the books and we took the card table out, in a case. I took it to the door. I called nineteen cabs and they wouldn't take it. Finally we got a cab, cost me two dollars and a half. We got it home. And after we had it home, I opened it up. It had a guarantee for thirty days. Guarantee. And after six months we sat down—we used to play Scrabble every night with the table there—we noticed that the table was wobbly. And then it got a little more wobbly, and finally one leg fell off.

5   So I wrote a letter to the company. I told them that my wife had been saving the plaid stamps for three years, and finally managed to get four and a half books. And we decided we're going to

get a card table. And I know that the guarantee was thirty days. But shortly after the guarantee ran out, the table started to get wobbly. The legs. And I wrote to Mister President—always write to the president of the company, never write to anybody else, only the president of the company, nobody else—and I said, I am eighty years of age, and my legs don't wobble. I said, After a while one leg fell off, and sir, I still have both of my legs. One of them hasn't fallen off yet. I said, Your table is built with steel piping all around. I said, You can rest assured that with this steel piping you could build a house on top of it. I said, I'm surprised that this happened. My wife and I would like to play Scrabble. So I said, We felt a little inconvenience—I took my family Bible, I put it on my knees to support the one corner of the table. But my wife, I said, objected to it. She said it was sacrilegious to do that. There we are, sir, I said, with all of our *Encyclopaedia Britannicas* on the floor, reaching all the way up—just enough to support one side.

6   Well, I don't remember every word I wrote, but the phone rang a couple of days afterwards. This was out in Detroit someplace, and somebody's voice says, "This is Miss Kelly, Mr. Scranton's secretary." President of the plaid stamps. "And as soon as he gets through laughing," she told us on the phone, "he's going to send you a card table." And sure enough, here it is. See?

III

7 What is being religious? Well, I think that my first analogy is as a child. My father and I were standing outside of our house, and a man passed by with his prayer shawl and a book under his arm, and he walked past us and said hello to my father. When he was out of sight, my father said to me, "He thinks he's religious. He's going to temple now to pray."

8   So we have people who wouldn't do you a kind thing, but they think they're religious because they go to synagogue every day. They'll stand outside this door here and won't open it because it's Saturday and they're not allowed to open a door, so they wait for you to open a door, see? But they wouldn't do a good turn for you, and that is what in my opinion being religious means.

9   As far as I'm concerned, I go to the synagogue maybe once a year on the holidays, and I buy two tickets because they charge. Did you ever hear that story of the fellow who tried to get in the synagogue? On a holiday, a high holiday. The fellow at the door said, "You can't go in." He said, "I got to go in. I just came from

California and I want to see my brother." So the fellow at the door says, "Well, go ahead, you can go in. But don't let me catch you praying."

10   So I go into synagogue and Henrietta joins me. And I sit down and I hear the rabbi deliver a sermon, which I don't hear too well. And I hear the choir. And I stay there a few hours till it's over. And I do this because I want to feel that innately I'm a Jew. And I want to feel that I still have my religious Jewish instincts. And I keep this up. And I'll do it as long as I can. But as far as being religious is concerned, I think I've gone out of my way to be kind to people, to do things for people, within my ability. And I think this is being religious. I believe in a God. Whether he believes in me, I don't know.

IV

11 I enjoy everything I do. I do it with enjoyment, for the simple reason that I don't do anything I don't enjoy. That's all. I do everything. Home here today, I vacuum and I even do the laundry. If it's necessary, I do ironing for my wife. And I don't mind doing that. I don't think anything is demeaning. I think that marriage is a partnership. We should help one another.

12   In this book I'm reading right now the author spends a couple of chapters talking about people who have jobs they don't like. But why don't they quit? People don't have the courage to quit. And do what they want to do. They should. If they have the courage. A lot of people have done so. Have quit their jobs and gone out and made good, doing what they want to do. But this requires courage. People are looking for security. They don't want to take a chance. . . .

13   I think I adopted new ideas as an entertainer, as a magician. I've adopted new ideas with new materials in art work, or new ideas of going and seeing others' art work and things like that. I think I have. I think that I can safely say that for an old man I'm not stagnant. I think most old people don't want to advance, don't want to learn anything new. I'm willing to learn something new.

V

14 Mrs. Roosevelt said that one of the unfortunate conditions of being old is losing your friends and your relatives. They pass away. And it's a natural thing. My wife is the only living relative of her family. Her entire family is gone, she's the only one left.

And I have lost so many of my old friends and relatives—and there's no replacement. You can't replace them because the new generation, new friends, new relatives, whatever, that you meet, they don't have the same background that you have—they can't go back all those years. Well, I just have to take it as it is. You just have to face it, that's all.

15   I don't think we have any control over life or destiny. It just happens. I have a situation right now that I'm trying to control. But I'm not dealing with it. Both of us were in the hospital. What if it happened again? What are we going to do? Or suppose we are incapacitated? I'm not dealing with the problem now and I should be. I don't think that I'm very bright not to consider it more seriously. And I feel a little conscience stricken that I'm not dealing with it. I don't think that I can deal with it religiously. I learned this in one little story. The rabbi sat next to the priest at the boxing match. And the fighters came in, and one of them got down on his knees and prayed before the fight, and the rabbi said to the priest, "Do you think that will help him?" And the priest said, "Yes, if he can fight."

A SECOND LOOK

1. Look again at paragraphs 10, 12, and 14. There are several signs that this is spoken English, not ordinary written English. What are some of these signs? Find other examples in the selection.

2. One of the most noticeable of Levy's characteristics is his sense of humor. Point out several examples.

3. What is Levy's attitude toward religion?

4. How do you think Levy views old age?

5. Levy admits that he is troubled by the thought that both he and his wife might become ill or incapacitated. Considering his personality, why do you think he is having trouble with this possibility.

IDEAS FOR WRITING

1. Here is a statement suggested by paragraph 11: "Theodore Levy is a man who enjoys whatever he does." Write a paragraph in which this

statement is the topic sentence. The rest of the paragraph should give examples (taken from the interview) showing that Levy enjoys a variety of things in his life.

2. Here is another statement suggested by paragraph 13: "Although he is nearing ninety, Theodore Levy has not grown stagnant." Write a paragraph using this statement as the topic sentence. The paragraph should give examples to show that Levy is a man who thinks clearly and uses his mind actively.

JOURNEY INTO OLD AGE

Pat Moore

LOOKING FORWARD

In an unusual experiment, twenty-six-year-old writer Pat Moore used makeup, wig, and clothes to pass for an eighty-five-year-old woman. In this essay, Moore explains what the transformation showed her about society's attitudes toward and its treatment of the elderly.

HELP WITH WORDS

apprehensive *(paragraph 1):* uneasy or fearful

gerontology *(paragraph 3):* science that deals with aging

incredibly *(paragraph 7):* unbelievably

condescended to *(paragraph 8):* treated as an inferior

dowdy *(paragraph 9):* not neat or stylish

quavered *(paragraph 10):* trembled

decipher *(paragraph 11):* to make out the meaning of

intimidated *(paragraph 17):* to be made timid or fearful

masquerade *(paragraph 18):* disguise

deteriorated *(paragraph 19):* run-down

verified *(paragraph 25):* found to be true

ironically *(paragraph 26):* differently from what was expected

musing *(paragraph 32):* meditating

rapport *(paragraph 32):* close relationship

traumas *(paragraph 34):* shocks

longevity *(paragraph 34):* long life

---

1   O n a May morning in 1979, I opened the door of my New York City apartment and stepped nervously into the hall. As an 85-year-old woman, I was apprehensive. I extended my cane, feeling carefully for the first step of the stairs. My legs strained awkwardly. One step . . . two . . . three . . . breathe hard . . . four. After 12 steps, I reached the first landing and leaned against the wall to catch my breath.

2   So far, so good, I said to myself. And then I stopped. Was I overdoing it? Would I really get away with this act? For I wasn't really 85. Underneath the trappings of my aged body was the real me, a 26-year-old woman.

3   I was pretending to be so much older because I wanted to find out what it is like to be elderly. As an industrial designer, I'd grown interested in the peculiar problems that some appliances present to older people. Eventually I enrolled in a gerontology course and, still wanting to know more, I finally decided to "become" an older person, to discover firsthand the problems faced by the elderly.

4   As a start I learned how to "age" myself—a complicated procedure requiring four hours. With latex foam giving my face its folds and wrinkles, a heavy fabric binding my body, and a gray wig on my head, I became 60 years older and ready to set forth on my grand adventure.

5   My destination that first day was a conference on aging in Columbus, Ohio. Out on the street I tried to signal a cab for the airport. Taxi after taxi flashed past, all empty. Did they feel that old ladies don't tip well? Finally one stopped.

6   At the airline ticket counter, I found myself in a line of young businessmen. "Good morning, sir!" the agent exclaimed brightly to each one. "Have a pleasant trip." When old-lady-me peered up at him through thick spectacles, however, all I got was a look at my ticket, a mutter of "Columbus" and an abrupt "Next."

7   The whole purpose of the conference, attended mostly by young professionals, was to study the problems of the elderly. Yet,

incredibly, the participants seemed to ignore the only "old lady" in their midst. When one of the young males offered coffee to a group of women, I found myself thinking, What about me? If I were young, he would offer me coffee too.

8   By day's end, I was angry. I had been condescended to, ignored, counted out in a way I had never known before. People, I felt, really do judge a book by its cover.

9   The experience was repeated in my neighborhood drugstore when, as a meek and dowdy old woman, I asked for a stomach medicine. The owner merely jerked a thumb over his shoulder. "Back there, bottom shelf."

10   Peering around, I quavered, "Can you help me find it?"

11   He looked up in annoyance, walked to the shelf and pointed down. I stooped to pick up a bottle and tried to decipher the small type. "Could you please read the directions for me?" I pleaded.

12   In irritation, he rattled them off, and then dismissed me with, "Okay, that it?" I was afraid to ask him anything more.

13   The next morning, I returned to the store as confident, 26-year-old Pat Moore.

14   "Good morning," the owner greeted me cheerfully. "How can we help you today?"

15   I used exactly the same words in asking for the stomach medicine.

16   "Oh," he said smiling, "it's right over here." Escorting me to the shelf, he kneeled down, picked up a bottle and carefully explained the directions, the sizes in which it came and the prices. Then he rang up the sale and wished me a fine day.

17   As I walked out of the store, my heart cried for the older woman. I could understand how she would become defensive and intimidated.

18   For three years I put on my masquerade at least one day a week, visiting 14 states, meeting hundreds of people. My experiences were varied—some bad, some good. I'll never forget the woman who held a heavy door open for me at a department store in Kansas City. When I thanked her, she gave me a quick hug and said, "I have a mother about your age in Fort Lauderdale. I just hope someone holds the door open for her."

19   But once, when I was foolishly walking alone in a deteriorated neighborhood at dusk, I was hurled to the ground by several laughing youngsters who beat me as they yanked away my purse. My mugging left me with a fractured wrist, a deep fear of being

out after dusk—and a clear idea of why the elderly often become housebound.

20   A few months later in a similar area, I was anxiously hobbling to catch a bus that was about to pull away. Suddenly a youngster raced toward me, and my heart stopped. Oh no, not again! Not in broad daylight! I cried inwardly.

21   Instead he ran up to alert the bus driver, who then waited for me. I felt as if the sun had come out from behind a thundercloud.

22   Many of my favorite encounters took place on park benches. As an 85-year-old, I could sit down beside an elderly person and easily strike up a conversation. We would just be two people enjoying the moment, the sunshine, the fresh air, without the pressure that I often felt as a 26-year-old go-getter. It made me a little envious that I wasn't a true member of their club.

23   In just that way I met an elderly man named George, who told me that for a year after his wife died he had sat alone in his apartment and cried. But then a friend accused him of acting like a spiteful child. "God has given you the incredible gift of life," the friend said, "and you're doing your best to make a mess of it!"

24   "Well," George said to me, "after that I got myself together. I made good friends, began to eat and exercise regularly, and soon I was feeling fine. You know," he said, slapping the bench in excitement, "it's just like I'm beginning to live all over again."

25   I could tell that George had taken a special interest in me, and it made me aware of a fact that I was to see verified again and again: we never grow old emotionally. We all want to be loved. Our bodies change, but our emotional needs do not.

26   Ironically, it was a child who helped unlock another secret of a serene old age. One afternoon I arrived at a hotel in Clearwater, Fla. Sweltering underneath my heavy makeup and wrappings, I could hardly wait to get to the beach. As I took my first breath of cool sea air, a tiny voice piped behind me.

27   "Would you like a cooky?"

28   I turned to see a little boy of about six. "No, thank you," I said suspecting that his sand-encrusted sack also carried frogs and other boy-treasures. His face darkened in disappointment. "On second thought," I told him, "I'd love a cooky."

29   He gave me a Fig Newton. "Do you like shells?" he asked.

30   "Yes, very much."

31   "I'll find you some." Then he put his hand in mine and led me down the golden beach. "There's one," he said. I started to lean

down. "Oh no, let me." Quickly picking it up, he brushed it off and slipped it into his sack. "I'll carry them for you."

32 So we made our way across the sand, the little boy bobbing with oohs and aahs at the shells he'd find, I musing about the mystic rapport that can grow between young and old. And I also saw that all of us, as we grow older, need to approach each day with a child's trust and innocence.

33 Now, five years after beginning my journey into old age, I have put away the gray wig, the makeup and trappings. I look at them with affection because I have learned so much through them.

34 The truly joyful people I met were always open to experience—yes, open to all the inevitable heartaches and illnesses and family traumas—yet they were the ones who faced life positively, proud of their longevity and of the experience and wisdom they had accumulated. Their self-esteem came from knowing they were much-loved children of God.

35 If I should be fortunate enough to become a real 85-year-old someday, I hope I'll have the friendliness and generosity and wide-eyed trust of my little friend on the beach. I'll also take a tip from my grandmother, who never even considered that she was old. As she told me once, "I've just lived longer than most people."

A SECOND LOOK

1. What is the chief device Moore uses to control the organization of this essay? Pick out some of the words and phrases that help the reader follow this pattern.

2. Is Moore's introduction clear and interesting? What about the information or writing determines this?

3. Good writing generally avoids clichés and time-worn proverbs, yet in paragraph 8 Moore writes: "People, I felt, really do judge a book by its cover." Is this a weakness or is the cliché effective in this case?

4. Overall, were Moore's experiences as an old lady negative or positive?

5. Moore says that her most revealing experience occurred when she met a little boy on the beach. Explain what she learned from him.

6. Moore claims that the "truly joyful people" she met were open to experiences, positive in their attitudes, and proud of their age. "Their self-esteem came from knowing they were much-loved children of God." Is this the conclusion you would draw from the experiences described in this essay?

IDEAS FOR WRITING

Pat Moore tried to identify with a group of people different from herself by literally "becoming" one of that group. Others have tried the same experiment, though generally for a shorter period of time. To understand the handicapped person's problems on the job, employers sometimes spend the day in a wheelchair or on crutches. Reporters have posed as prisoners and allowed themselves to be locked up to get realistic material for their stories. Students take over the jobs of local officials for a day to learn what their jobs are like. You can probably think of more examples of literal identification with others to improve understanding.

To prepare for this writing assignment, choose someone who is different from yourself in a particular way. If possible, spend some time observing the person. Note as many details as possible about how the person speaks, moves, dresses, or talks. Try to identify with the person. Try to decide what the person's thoughts and feelings are as you observe him or her.

When you have finished collecting details from your observation, write an account of several hours in that person's life. Use "I" in your essay, but write as if you were the other person, not yourself. In your account, try to reveal the other person's thoughts and attitudes.

WHISPER THE PAST

Ryan Hardesty

LOOKING FORWARD

Ryan Hardesty, a freshman composition student, wrote the following essay when he was asked to describe a place he knew well. The essay focuses on a decaying tipple in the middle of an abandoned coal field, but his description does more than help the reader understand what the tipple is and how it looks. Notice the frequent comparisons between the condition of the tipple now and the role it played in the past.

HELP WITH WORDS

accusation *(paragraph 2):* a claim of fault or wrongdoing
predominant *(paragraph 4):* having the most influence
meager *(paragraph 4):* of poor quality
symbolized *(paragraph 4):* stood for
symbol *(paragraph 4):* a representative
erupts *(paragraph 5):* breaks out
precariously *(paragraph 6):* insecurely
overwrought *(paragraph 7):* overly excited

inevitable *(paragraph 9):* unavoidable

dissolution *(paragraph 9):* breakup

---

1   I watch in silence as the evening wind gains force, causing monstrous black clouds of coal dust to rise and swirl and fall again.

2   I'm sitting on a half-buried iron beam. An unknown length of the beam lies deep beneath a pile of crumbled coal; three feet of it extend into the air like some skeletal finger, pointing to the old tipple in a quiet accusation. The area before me is nothing more than a level field covered by a foot-thick blanket of finely crushed coal and mud. Here and there a few scrawny weeds struggle hopelessly to survive in the black, mushy ground. The wind, now only a whisper, brushes these tiny weeds gently as it passes. Apart from the wind, there is only silence.

3   Over there, across this barren field, stands the tipple.

4   In my great-grandfather's day—and still today—these tipples were buildings for cleaning and crushing the coal that black-faced miners had painfully cut. In those days they used picks and shovels and muscles. Now they use giant metal monsters called "machines." Numerous tipples dotted the landscape, and they were the predominant figure in every person's meager life. The tipples symbolized hard work and prosperity (what pitifully little there was). Every man in the community, my great-grandfather included, worked in the tipple or in one of the many coal mines nearby; and every person owed his livelihood, either directly or indirectly, to this dark and dismal, constantly busy piece of metal. The tipple was the physical symbol of a unique way of life. This building before me once loomed large in the lives of my ancestors.

5   Today the tipple stands in stony silence, unused and abandoned, lonely and forgotten, old and decaying. Thirty rusted orange legs of metal rise from the dark ground, thrusting their way fifty feet into the air. Each sturdy leg stands ten feet or more from the others. This permitted smoke-belching locomotives and long lines of dull black railroad cars to pass between them. The main building sits comfortably atop these legs, the way a black widow crouches on her legs in some quiet corner. The tipple is a

roughly rectangular, five-story metal box coated with layers of faded blue tin. At one corner of the tipple, a narrow conveyor belt worms its way into the unseen depths of the building. At one time it carried freshly mined coal to the eagerly waiting machines inside. At another corner a second conveyor belt erupts from an opening in the blue skin of the tipple, carrying useless rock and slate away to be loaded into trucks. At one time all of this was new and brightly shining in the sun.

6   Now, amid the shadows of evening, the once mighty tipple slowly falls apart. The smell of decay hangs heavily on the air— the smell of rusty metal and thick, dry coal dust, the smell of grease and oil and smoke, the smell of emptiness and long disuse. Here a bundle of mud-covered pipes hangs limp and lifeless, swaying gently back and forth with a faint creaking sound. There a stairway has broken free of its former hold against the back wall of the tipple and droops precariously to one side. Everywhere there are broken beams and rails and windows, blue tin doors strangely ajar, stairways twisted and mangled, oddly shaped bits of rusty metal littering the ground, and clear water dripping rhythmically from large holes in the tipple floor. Far above my head, in the deeply shadowed face of the tipple, two square pieces of tin have somehow come unattached and fallen to the ground, leaving two large spaces of darkness that look like dying eyes.

7   Suddenly, either through a curious trick of shadow or an over-wrought imagination, the front side of the tipple becomes a grinning, blue-faced corpse, a malformed skull, a dead and crumbling shell that once hummed with life and energy. Those distant holes of blackness look like rotting eyes, and that row of double windows just beneath them seems to be a toothless, lipless mouth. It grins horribly as it steadily falls back into nothingness. It screams as it dies.

8   I have stumbled upon a corpse! This dingy-looking tipple is in fact a corpse! Over the past fifty years it has decayed slowly, yet steadily, like all good corpses should. Even now, as my great-grandfather's corpse lies painlessly beneath the angry earth, rotting away to the dust from which it sprang, the soulless monster that crushed his body and his spirit stands above the coal-covered ground, falling gradually back into the nothingness from which it was created.

9   My great-grandfather died long ago, and with him died an

entire breed of men and a brutally wonderful way of life. All that remains of those forever dead times is a crumbling blue ruin, standing silently in an empty field, awaiting its own inevitable dissolution. When the tipple is gone, only my memories shall remain. And when I die, the tipple will die, my great-grandfather will die, the past will die. They shall speak no more.

A SECOND LOOK

1. The last four sentences of paragraph 5 alternate two introductory phrases. What effect does this repetition have?

2. Paragraphs 7 and 8 develop two comparisons. What are they?

3. In paragraphs 4 and 5, Hardesty sets up a contrast between the tipple he sees now and the tipple as it was in his great-grandfather's lifetime. Try to restate in a few sentences the primary differences he emphasizes.

4. This essay is a meditation, an account of the author's thoughts and feelings as he views a scene. From his description, decide how Hardesty feels about the tipple and the coalfields.

IDEAS FOR WRITING

Choose some place that you are already familiar with and can revisit now. Go there and sit for at least an hour, making notes on what you see, hear, smell, and so forth. Record your reactions to what is going on around you. Observe closely and take notes on everything in the area.

As you take notes, include details about the appearance of the place, the furnishings around you, the main colors you see, the people or objects there. Include information about your own reactions. Do you find the place pleasant, unpleasant, interesting, boring, thought-provoking?

When you have finished your notes, reread them several times to see whether they contain some kind of pattern. Perhaps most of the details can be grouped under two or three headings, while others can be dropped from the list. Continue to work with your notes to discover some thought about the place that could form the main idea of an essay. Write an introduction in which you state this main idea; then develop the rest of the paper from the material in your notes.

MAKING CONNECTIONS

Pat Moore describes herself as an older person with words that emphasize her weakness and helplessness. She says she was "meek and dowdy," her voice "quavered," and when she asked for help she "pleaded" (paragraphs 9, 10, and 11). This language suggests an attitude toward age that may have influenced what Moore experienced. Look for other places in the text that help us understand Moore's attitude toward age. Compare this attitude with Theodore Levy's in *Until the Singing Stops*.

Louise Bernikow is writing of being older rather than elderly, but would you predict that her attitude toward being elderly would be more like Moore's or Levy's?

HEROISM

WHERE HAVE ALL THE HEROES GONE?

Pete Axthelm

LOOKING FORWARD

In this essay about heroism, Pete Axthelm not only identifies heroes from the past, he also considers whether our modern society is capable of producing twentieth-century heroes. He points out that most Americans are suspicious of courageous deeds and that the media are fast to expose any flaws of so-called heroes. Nevertheless, Americans still respect heroism and admire bravery and daring whenever they find true examples of it.

HELP WITH WORDS

unabashed *(paragraph 2):* unashamed, unembarrassed

carping *(paragraph 2):* finding fault

martial *(paragraph 2):* warlike

alleged *(paragraph 2):* assumed but not proven

technocrats *(paragraph 2):* specialists in technology

scrutinize *(paragraph 3):* look closely at

barrage *(paragraph 3):* heavy artillery fire

bureaucrats *(paragraph 4):* officials who follow routine

legions *(paragraph 4):* large groups

prattle *(paragraph 4):* talk foolishly

elusive *(paragraph 5):* hard to define

chic *(paragraph 6):* fashionable

segment *(paragraph 6):* a part

artifacts *(paragraph 7):* manmade objects, especially very old ones

reputedly *(paragraph 7):* according to popular belief

stark *(paragraph 7):* extremely simple

idiom *(paragraph 11):* a style of speaking

Be Silent, Friend
Here Heroes Died
To Blaze A Trail
For Other Men

1   Near that sign at the door of the Alamo, there are several simpler warnings. NO SMOKING. QUIET. GENTLEMEN REMOVE HATS. I did not see anyone light up inside the Alamo. There were few noises except for the subdued and reverent words of the tour guides. The gentlemen were all bareheaded. And somehow these minor gestures of respect seemed important. Standing in a dusty courtyard in the dry Texas heat, in a season when Americans were knifing one another over tanks of gasoline, I felt refreshed to be in a place where the memory of heroism and trailblazing can still make a friend take off his hat.

2   I have been reading quite a bit lately about how America has grown too rich, too confused or too sophisticated for heroes. John Wayne is gone, his larger-than-life adventures replaced mainly by movies that offer only blinding special effects or characters trying to find themselves. Even when a rare film like "The Deer Hunter" attempts to portray an unabashed war hero, nobody notices: The critical reaction is mainly carping about its martial philosophy or alleged racism. Sports stars, once expected to embody heroism as well as talent, have lost much of their luster and our trust in a flurry of team-hopping and renegotiation of contracts. The astronauts have been smugly dismissed as technocrats, their heritage reduced to a nervous summer of Skylab

jokes. Once, we routinely asked our kids who their heroes were. Today we fumble for answers when they ask us if there are any heroes left.

3   Vietnam and Watergate played their part in all this, as we learned to beware our leaders and to scrutinize them, warts and all. The media have done so with a vengeance, and few leaders can stand up to the barrage. But a cynical age now accepts the tarnished coin of celebrity in place of heroic virtue—and thus the best-seller lists are filled with books by Watergate felons and their co-conspirators.

4   **Destiny:** I am not convinced of the impossibility of modern heroism. Anyone who has met the coal miners of eastern Kentucky or the firemen of the South Bronx would be foolish to proclaim the death of self-sacrifice or bravery—qualities that surely have some relation to heroism. Can an era be hopelessly bleak and unheroic when two young journalists can help to bring down a corrupt administration and a few bureaucrats stand up to expose the waste and carelessness of the bureaucracies that they serve? Even in a troubled land of cookie-cutter shopping malls and thought-deadening discos, I suspect there are a few people who still seek out the lonely roads, take the personal risks and dare to shape their world. While modern legions may prattle about human potential, those few actually fulfill it. And call it destiny.

5   Before trying to define or search for heroism, I wanted to reach out and touch that elusive quality. Surely men touched it at Valley Forge or San Juan Hill, on the Bad Lands of the frontier or the Sea of Tranquillity. But few felt it on more intimate terms than the Texas freedom fighters of the 1830s. So the Alamo seemed as good a place as any to make a start.

6   Some visitors have been disappointed by this small, modest shrine in the midst of downtown San Antonio. Today, the Alamo must battle for tourists' attention against the chic Riverwalk and teeming streets nearby. On a corner a block away, for example, a large sign over a servicemen's Christian center proclaims: RIGHTEOUSNESS EXALTETH A NATION. I did not see any servicemen in the center as I passed. But at night, a segment of the city's large hooker population works that corner. I asked one girl there about the Alamo. "I'm from Miami, what do I know about that crap?" she said. "You ain't another one of those John Wayne freaks, are you?" An unpromising backdrop for history.

7   But the Alamo overcomes. In its resistance to the vast scale of Texas, it asserts a stubborn grandeur of its own. Its artifacts are simple, its tone understated. In one display case is a rifle with which Davy Crockett reputedly killed 350 bears in one summer. "That's only a legend, of course," tour guide Lupe Nava warns softly. "But Crockett was such a good marksman that it could be true." The heroes, Crockett and Jim Bowie and commanding officer William Travis and the rest, are never oversold here. In merciful contrast to the stars of other modern tourist attractions, they are never depicted in life-size "multimedia presentations" that can only serve to cut the subjects down to size. Their story is stark, their memory vivid on its own terms. I think there are some lessons in this. . . .

8   An independent Republic of Texas was what the heroes of the Alamo wanted. The price was their lives, and the odds against them were about 30 to 1. They knew the odds and played out the deadly game. But they fought so bravely that Santa Anna's huge Mexican Army was weakened. Forty-six days after the fall of the Alamo in 1836, another Texas army routed the Mexicans at San Jacinto. The Alamo had been remembered and avenged, and Texas was free. In death, the heroes of the Alamo had reshaped their world. In doing so, they had taken a fierce self-respect to the level of heroism—and provided a working definition that endures and illuminates.

9   Some comparisons are irresistible. Jim Bowie, among the oldest Alamo fighters at forty-one, was a wealthy landowner with connections in high places. Today, when the lower classes do our fighting and wealth and connections smooth many a journey through politics or business, it may be hard to grasp the ideals that drove Bowie to the Texas war—and kept him there even after he was stricken with typhoid pneumonia. Bowie died, his famous knife bloodied, while fighting from his sickbed. . . .

10   James Butler Bonham was a courier who left the Alamo during the siege and rode to Goliad, ninety-five miles away, to plead for reinforcement. He is less known than Crockett or Bowie, but his horse, it seems to me, should gallop through our modern consciousness. . . . The commander at Goliad could offer no troops. At that moment, Bonham knew that the Alamo was doomed. But he turned around, fought his way back through the Mexican Army and rejoined his comrades to fight to a certain death.

11   **Challenge:** No one faced the odds more squarely than

Bonham. No one had more options. Already a hero, he could have joined other Texas forces, fought to other glories, grabbed a few more days or years for a life that ended at twenty-nine. In the modern idiom that replaces self-respect with self-serving, he could have coped. It is difficult even to speculate on the depths of Bonham's dedication. Perhaps modern analysts would speak of obsession, self-destructive tendencies, [or] male bonding among heroes. But the hoofbeats of Bonham's ride express it much better. They leave us with the lingering and essential challenge: Who among modern heroes would have made that return trip? . . .

12 **Human Nature:** On my way home from the Alamo, I stopped in Nashville to talk with songwriter Tom T. Hall, whose country music salutes countless everyday heroes. "I think that heroism is basic to human nature," Hall said. "We look at Martin Luther King or the Pope going into Communist Poland, and we can't really avoid the possibilities of heroism. Maybe our own kind takes a much smaller form, like going into a mine shaft every morning or making the refrigerator payments in time to keep a family eating. But it's there. Given the chance, I think a lot of guys in mines or factories would make that ride back into the Alamo."

13 Those words may be hard to believe. But to stop believing them would be like smoking in the Alamo. To deny modern heroism, it seems to me, is to admit that the odds are too long, the game no longer worth playing. Without heroes, we lose something of ourselves. I do not believe that we will ever accept that loss without listening one more time for hoofbeats.

A SECOND LOOK

1. What typical sources of heroism does Axthelm mention in paragraph 2? Why are these heroes no longer acceptable?

2. In what ways have the Vietnam War and the Watergate scandal influenced Americans' attitudes toward heroes?

3. Axthelm singles out James Butler Bonham for special notice. Why should Bonham be considered more courageous than the other fighters at the Alamo?

4. In explaining Bonham's options, Axthelm says, "he could have coped." What does the popular word *coped* mean in this sentence?

5. Why does Axthelm frequently mention the hoofbeats of Bonham's horse? (See paragraphs 10, 11, and 13.)

6. Review the characteristics of the Alamo fighters mentioned in paragraph 8 and then write the definition of *heroism* that this paragraph suggests.

IDEAS FOR WRITING

In groups assigned by your instructor, write down the names of as many modern heroes as you can think of. Give reasons for your choices. (Remember that Axthelm mentions self-sacrifice and bravery as heroic qualities.) Then select one of the names and write a paper in which you explain why you think this individual is a modern hero. If you need to know more about the person you choose, you might check the library for further information. Your instructor or a librarian can suggest useful sources of material.

THE CROSS OF CESAR CHAVEZ

Stan Steiner

LOOKING FORWARD

In this chapter from his book *La Raza*, Stan Steiner explains step by step how Cesar Chavez carried out a twenty-five-day fast to call attention to the problems of poor farm workers in Southern California. You should not only notice what Chavez did during each part of the fast but also decide what he believed the significance of his actions to be.

HELP WITH WORDS

portentous *(paragraph 1):* significant; suggesting future events

ultimate *(paragraph 2):* extreme, in the highest degree

Forty Acres *(paragraph 3):* land bought in 1966 by the National Farm Workers Union to be the headquarters of the movement

pilgrimage *(paragraph 4):* a journey to a religious shrine

barrios (paragraph 4): Chicano sections of cities

campesinos (paragraph 6): farm workers

huelga (paragraph 6): literally "strike" in Spanish; also stands for the migrant workers' movement

desecrated *(paragraph 11):* treated with disrespect

1   The sacrifice of Cesar Chavez began during Lent, in the chill spring of 1968. It was tragic and portentous. He offered his body in a "Lenten Fast for Peace and Nonviolence" that lasted for twenty-five days. He sacrificed one-fifth of his flesh, thirty-five pounds, to "the pain and suffering of the farm workers." Except for a few ounces of bouillon and a few mouthfuls of unsweetened grapefruit juice ordered by his doctor, for twenty-five days he had nothing but water. He grew so weak he could hardly talk or walk.

2   He fasted because self-sacrifice was "the ultimate act of manliness," Chavez said. He fasted because "my heart was filled with grief when I saw the pain" of his people in the fields. He fasted for nonviolence.

3   An altar was built in the garage of the union's cooperative gas station, on the Forty Acres. Hundreds of farm workers came from the fields to pray every day. The altar, on the back of a truck, became a shrine.

4   Chavez sat in the unheated, unfinished garage and prayed and shivered. The Holy Mass that was celebrated every day for his sacrificial act became the scene of a pilgrimage. Women brought candles and offerings. The men knelt in the dirt by the hundreds, coming from the barrios, the remote country crossroads, the migrant camps.

5   On the fourth day of his fast, the land-grant leader of New Mexico, Reies Tijerina, came to pray. Chavez and Tijerina embraced.

6   In a rally of farm workers—though he was becoming weak—Chavez appealed for funds for the defense of the fiery land-grant leader who had been arrested for kidnaping, murder, and insurrection. The poor campesinos contributed five hundred dollars, and Chavez gave Tijerina a huge red huelga flag, which Tijerina draped over his shoulders like a prayer shawl.

7   On the thirteenth day of his fast, Chavez, by now quite pale, was himself taken before Superior Court Justice Martin Baker to reply to charges of violation of court injunctions in the strike against Guimarra Vineyards. The growers had filed a complaint of twelve charges. Well over one thousand farm workers overflowed the courtroom in Bakersfield, its corridors, and the outside plaza. Judge Baker postponed the hearing, and Chavez returned to the altar in the garage.

8   On the twenty-fifth day, he broke his fast by breaking bread with the late Senator Robert Kennedy, who flew to Delano to be beside his friend.

9   Ten thousand farm workers and their families gathered before the altar in the cold March sun. Some say it was the largest meeting of farm workers in the history of the Southwest. Beneath the wooden cross that had been carried on the union's Pilgrimage to Sacramento, and the banner of the Virgin of Guadalupe, with rows of red flags of the huelga whirling in the wind, Robert Kennedy rose to say that by his sacrifice Cesar Chavez had told the world that "violence is no answer."...

10   On the site of the fast of Cesar Chavez, they erected a huge cross made of telephone poles. The cross towered for thirty feet above the barren land, vines grew up on it and flowers were attached to it. Under the cross they held religious ceremonies, open-air masses, and the sunrise service at Easter. Vandals tried twice to burn the cross to the ground. Its wood withstood the fires, and the charred symbol of nonviolence remained visible for miles.

11   The cross of Cesar Chavez was desecrated the week before the Fourth of July. It was cut by a power saw and fell in the dust and the weeds.

A SECOND LOOK

1. Steiner organizes his work according to the order in which the events occurred. What words or phrases help the reader to follow the progress of the fast?

2. Notice the details describing the final day of the fast. Does Robert Kennedy's involvement in the final day help or detract from Chavez's purpose? Why do you think so?

3. Chavez began his fast during Lent. Why is this an appropriate time for the protest? Pick out other religious activities of Chavez and the workers. Why does the author emphasize these?

4. The title of the essay comes from events described in the last two paragraphs. What does the association of a cross with Chavez suggest about his fast?

IDEAS FOR WRITING

1. Choose any event that you know a lot about. It could be an historical incident, a strike at a factory, a training program for the Army Reserves, or whatever. The event should cover several days, and you should be able to list all parts of it. Then, from your list, write a clear account of what happened. Use linking words or phrases such as *then, afterward, three days later,* and so forth, so that someone not familiar with the event can follow the action.

2. Steiner's account of Cesar Chavez suggests that self-sacrifice is a major quality of heroism. Think of someone you know or know of who willingly made a sacrifice for someone else. Write a brief description of this person. Begin by explaining who the person is. Then show step by step what sacrifice this person made and tell who benefited from it.

I KNOW WHY THE CAGED BIRD SINGS

Maya Angelou

LOOKING FORWARD

Maya Angelou has established a wide reputation as a singer and actress as well a writer. In this chapter from her autobiography, Angelou recalls the suspense and excitement in a small town in Arkansas over Joe Louis's match to keep the title of world heavy-weight champion. Notice the ways in which Angelou shows the reader the importance of the match before she states this main idea directly.

HELP WITH WORDS

apprehensive *(paragraph 2):* fearful

cracker *(paragraph 3):* slang for a white person

assent *(paragraph 10):* approval

"master's voice" *(paragraph 12):* part of an advertising slogan for RCA radios and phonographs

maimed *(paragraph 16):* wounded or crippled

accusations *(paragraph 17):* charges

ordained *(paragraph 17):* divinely ordered

hewers *(paragraph 17):* cutters

ambrosia *(paragraph 27):* food for the gods

white lightning *(paragraph 27):* moonshine, homemade whiskey

---

1   The last inch of space was filled, yet people continued to wedge themselves along the walls of the Store. Uncle Willie had turned the radio up to its last notch so that youngsters on the porch wouldn't miss a word. Women sat on kitchen chairs, dining room chairs, stools and upturned wooden boxes. Small children and babies perched on every lap available and men leaned on the shelves or on each other.

2   The apprehensive mood was shot through with shafts of gaiety, as a black sky is streaked with lightning.

3   "I ain't worried 'bout this fight. Joe's gonna whip that cracker like it's open season."

4   "He gone whip him till that white boy call him Momma."

5   At last the talking was finished and the string-along songs about razor blades were over and the fight began.

6   "A quick jab to the head." In the Store the crowd grunted. "A left to the head and a right and another left." One of the listeners cackled like a hen and was quieted.

7   "They're in a clench, Louis is trying to fight his way out."

8   Some bitter comedian on the porch said, "That white man don't mind hugging that niggah now, I betcha."

9   "The referee is moving in to break them up, but Louis finally pushed the contender away and it's an uppercut to the chin. The contender is hanging on, now he's backing away. Louis catches him with a short left to the jaw."

10   A tide of murmuring assent poured out the doors and into the yard.

11   "Another left and another left. Louis is saving that mighty right. . . ." The mutter in the Store had grown into a baby roar and it was pierced by the clang of a bell and the announcer's "That's the bell for round three, ladies and gentlemen."

12   As I pushed my way into the Store I wondered if the announcer gave any thought to the fact that he was addressing as "ladies and gentlemen" all the Negroes around the world who sat sweating and praying, glued to their "master's voice."

13   There were only a few calls for RC Colas, Dr. Peppers, and Hire's root beer. The real festivities would begin after the fight. Then even the old Christian ladies who taught their children and tried themselves to practice turning the other cheek would buy soft drinks, and if the Brown Bomber's victory was a particularly bloody one they would order peanut patties and Baby Ruths also.

14   Bailey and I lay the coins on top of the cash register. Uncle Willie didn't allow us to ring up sales during a fight. It was too noisy and might shake up the atmosphere. When the gong rang for the next round we pushed through the near-sacred quiet to the herd of children outside.

15   "He's got Louis against the ropes and now it's a left to the body and a right to the ribs. Another right to the body, it looks like it was low. . . . Yes, ladies and gentlemen, the referee is signaling, but the contender keeps raining the blows on Louis. It's another to the body, and it looks like Louis is going down."

16   My race groaned. It was our people falling. It was another lynching, yet another Black man hanging on a tree. One more woman ambushed and raped. A Black boy whipped and maimed. It was hounds on the trail of a man running through slimy swamps. It was a white woman slapping her maid for being forgetful.

17   The men in the Store stood away from the walls and at attention. Women greedily clutched the babes on their laps while on the porch the shufflings and smiles, flirtings and pinching of a few minutes before were gone. This might be the end of the world. If Joe lost we were back in slavery and beyond help. It would all be true, the accusations that we were lower types of human beings. Only a little higher than the apes. True that we were stupid and ugly and lazy and dirty and, unlucky and worst of all, that God Himself hated us and ordained us to be hewers of wood and drawers of water, forever and ever, world without end.

18   We didn't breathe. We didn't hope. We waited.

19   "He's off the ropes, ladies and gentlemen. He's moving towards the center of the ring." There was no time to be relieved. The worst might still happen.

20   "And now it looks like Joe is mad. He's caught Carnera with a left hook to the head and a right to the head. It's a left jab to the body and another left to the head. There's a left cross and a right to the head. The contender's right eye is bleeding and he can't seem to keep his block up. Louis is penetrating every block. The

referee is moving in, but Louis sends a left to the body and it's the uppercut to the chin and the contender is dropping. He's on the canvas, ladies and gentlemen."

21 Babies slid to the floor as women stood up and men leaned toward the radio.

22 "Here's the referee. He's counting. One, two, three, four, five, six, seven . . . Is the contender trying to get up again?"

23 All the men in the Store shouted, "NO."

24 "—eight, nine, ten." There were a few sounds from the audience, but they seemed to be holding themselves in against tremendous pressure.

25 "The fight is all over, ladies and gentlemen. Let's get the microphone over to the referee. . . . Here he is. He's got the Brown Bomber's hand, he's holding it up. . . . Here he is. . . ."

26 Then the voice, husky and familiar, came to wash over us— "The winnah, and still heavyweight champeen of the world . . . Joe Louis."

27 Champion of the world. A Black boy. Some Black mother's son. He was the strongest man in the world. People drank Coca-Colas like ambrosia and ate candy bars like Christmas. Some of the men went behind the Store and poured white lightning in their soft-drink bottles, and a few of the bigger boys followed them. Those who were not chased away came back blowing their breath in front of themselves like proud smokers.

28 It would take an hour or more before the people would leave the Store and head for home. Those who lived too far had made arrangements to stay in town. It wouldn't do for a Black man and his family to be caught on a lonely country road on a night when Joe Louis had proved that we were the strongest people in the world.

A SECOND LOOK

1. Sometimes a writer deliberately exaggerates or overstates in order to make a point. Find several examples of such exaggeration in Angelou's narrative.

2. Why is Louis's victory so important to the listeners in the country store?

3. When we expect characters to behave in a certain way, but their behavior turns out to be the opposite of what we expect, that is one kind of *irony*. Explain the irony in paragraphs 13 and 28.

IDEAS FOR WRITING

1. Choose one of the following statements:

   "Even though they play for fame and money, professional athletes can be real heroes."

   "Professional athletes are in sports for the fame and money; they should not be considered real heroes."

   Use the statement you choose as the main idea in an essay. Support your opinion with examples of sports figures you feel are or are not heroic. Remember that you must make your idea of "hero" clear before you can show that professional athletes do or do not qualify. Assume that your readers have not yet made up their minds on this issue. You must convince them.

2. Write a paragraph or two in which you describe the tension and excitement of the crowd just before a sports event begins. The writing will be much easier if you have a specific event in mind and let the reader know what it is. Here is a sample topic sentence: "Just before the tip-off of the city basketball championship game, energy surged through the crowd like electricity."

STRIDE TOWARD FREEDOM

Martin Luther King, Jr.

LOOKING FORWARD

In these paragraphs, Martin Luther King, Jr., who was himself a hero and probably the greatest leader in the history of the American civil rights movement, describes a simple action that many people saw as an act of heroism—a black woman refusing to give up her seat to a white man on a Montgomery bus. At the same time, Reverend King is explaining why something happened, because this action marked the beginning of the famous Montgomery bus boycott. For days the blacks of Montgomery, Alabama, refused to ride the public buses, leaving them nearly empty. This became a turning point in the civil rights movement, but its beginning was a single, brave act.

HELP WITH WORDS

speculation *(paragraph 2):* an opinion formed without enough evidence

plausible *(paragraph 2):* believable

persistent *(paragraph 2):* occurring again and again

invariable *(paragraph 2):* unchanging

unwarranted *(paragraph 3):* without foundation; undeserved

intrepid *(paragraph 3):* fearless

affirmation *(paragraph 3):* a strong positive statement

accumulated *(paragraph 3):* piled up

indignities *(paragraph 3):* disgraces, humiliations

aspirations *(paragraph 3):* desires, ambitions

impeccable *(paragraph 4):* without fault

---

1   On December 1, 1955, an attractive Negro seamstress, Mrs. Rosa Parks, boarded the Cleveland Avenue bus in downtown Montgomery. She was returning home after her regular day's work in the Montgomery Fair—a leading department store. Tired from long hours on her feet, Mrs. Parks sat down in the first seat behind the section reserved for whites. Not long after she took her seat, the bus operator ordered her, along with three other Negro passengers, to move back in order to accommodate boarding white passengers. By this time every seat in the bus was taken. This meant that if Mrs. Parks followed the driver's command she would have to stand while a white male passenger, who had just boarded the bus, would sit. The other three Negro passengers immediately complied with the driver's request. But Mrs. Parks quietly refused. The result was her arrest.

2   There was to be much speculation about why Mrs. Parks did not obey the driver. Many people in the white community argued that she had been "planted" by the NAACP in order to lay the groundwork for a test case, and at first glance that explanation seemed plausible, since she was a former secretary of the local branch of the NAACP. So persistent and persuasive was this argument that it convinced many reporters from all over the country. Later on, when I was having press conferences three times a week—in order to accommodate the reporters and journalists who came to Montgomery from all over the world—the invariable first question was: "Did the NAACP start the bus boycott?"

3   But the accusation was totally unwarranted, as the testimony of both Mrs. Parks and the officials of the NAACP revealed. Actually, no one can understand the action of Mrs. Parks unless he realizes that eventually the cup of endurance runs over, and the human personality cries out, "I can take it no longer." Mrs.

Parks's refusal to move back was her intrepid affirmation that she had had enough. It was an individual expression of a timeless longing for human dignity and freedom. She was not "planted" there by the NAACP, or any other organization; she was planted there by her personal sense of dignity and self-respect. She was anchored to that seat by the accumulated indignities of days gone by and the boundless aspirations of generations yet unborn. She was a victim of both the forces of history and the forces of destiny. She had been tracked down by the Zeitgeist—the spirit of the time.

4   Fortunately, Mrs. Parks was ideal for the role assigned to her by history. She was a charming person with a radiant personality, soft spoken and calm in all situations. Her character was impeccable and her dedication deep-rooted. All of these traits together made her one of the most respected people in the Negro community.

A SECOND LOOK

1. King's essay (of which this is the beginning) shows cause and effect: Mrs. Parks's arrest was a cause; the bus boycott was the effect. He also shows cause-and-effect relationships in paragraphs 1 and 3. What are they?

2. Near the end of paragraph 3, King emphasizes the importance of his point by attracting our attention with repetition. Find several examples. Would even more repetition be effective? Why or why not?

3. In paragraph 1, King tells us a good deal about Mrs. Parks, mentioning her appearance, occupation, place of employment, and so forth. Since it is her action that becomes important, why does King give so much personal information about her? Is this a successful writing technique?

4. Moving from a bus seat may seem a small matter. Why did Mrs. Parks choose to go to jail rather than leave her seat?

5. King says that Mrs. Parks was "tracked down by . . . the spirit of the time." Why was the time right for an action such as hers?

IDEAS FOR WRITING

1. Sometimes a personal event such Mrs. Parks's refusal to move or Joe Louis's fight or Cesar Chavez's fast can take on importance for large groups of people. More recent examples might include U.S. Olympic victories over Russian teams or the flight of the first American woman astronaut. In small groups or as a class, discuss other examples. You might include anything from a nuclear protest to an athletic victory. The only condition is that the events you name must have taken on importance for a group beyond the individuals involved, making those individuals heroic.

   Choose one of these events as the subject of an essay. When you write, first describe the event for the readers who may not be familiar with it. Tell about the person or persons involved. Explain clearly what they did. Then go on to show your readers why this event was important to others and why those you are writing about became heroes.

2. Complete the following sentence: "I would rather go to jail than _____." Then write a paragraph using this statement as the topic sentence and explaining why you feel so strongly about your subject.

MAKING CONNECTIONS

At one point Axthelm says of the Alamo heroes that in death they "reshaped their world" and in the process provided a working definition of heroism by which we still measure heroes (paragraph 8). Still, Joe Louis and Rosa Parks seem heroic without facing death. Cesar Chavez was willing to suffer a fast, but he took bouillon and grapefruit juice when he was at the point of starvation. How can heroism be defined to include various types of heroes?

WOMEN AND MEN

YES, WOMEN AND MEN CAN BE "JUST FRIENDS"

Marjorie Franco

LOOKING FORWARD

In this essay, Marjorie Franco begins with examples from her youth and builds up to the main idea, which is stated in paragraph 5. She shows by the arrangement of her ideas that men and women must first establish their own identities before they can form real friendships.

HELP WITH WORDS

platonic *(paragraph 3):* free from sexual desire

mutual *(paragraph 4):* common or shared

astounded *(paragraph 4):* shocked or amazed

psychotherapist *(paragraph 5):* one who treats psychological disorders

siblings *(paragraph 5):* brothers and sisters

discomfiting *(paragraph 6):* confusing

1   I remember a summer day when I was ten years old: I was walking my dog, Lucky, in the South Side Chicago neighborhood where I grew up. Lucky strained at his leash, sniffing the trunk of the neighborhood's favorite climbing tree. Suddenly a wild shout startled me: "Look out, Rehn Peterson's sister!" and I saw Teddy Wilson, my brother's friend, on his Silver King bicycle, bearing down on me at top speed. With great presence of mind I leaped aside and, to Lucky's astonishment, slammed hard against the tree. I was furious—not because I'd been very nearly run down by a bike, and not because I'd had the wind knocked out of me by a tree. I was outraged because Teddy Wilson had denied me my identity.

2   On that day something stirred in me. Until then I had given little thought to who I was. My brother, two years older, was close to me; I was his friend and I knew it. He had other friends, of course, boys—they were always around—and because I was my brother's friend I had assumed I was their friend, too. But on that summer day, in the eyes of Teddy Wilson, I was "Rehn Peterson's sister" and nothing more.

3   But I wanted more. And in the years that followed, because of that drive for identity, I gained some practical experience in platonic friendship. Never mind that my girlfriend Florence, who read *True Story*, had whispered hotly into my ear, "Boys have uncontrollable passions, and they can't help it." I hadn't noticed any uncontrollable passion, unless you want to count the time Teddy Wilson said I looked fat in my bathing suit, and in that case the uncontrollable passion was mine.

4   I became friends with my brother's boyfriends and remained so until we all grew up and scattered from the neighborhood. As a friend, I went with Roy to his senior prom because his girlfriend was out of town; I went to plays with Elmer because we had developed a mutual interest in the theatre; I learned to cook with Jack since we both liked to cook (we experimented in our parents' kitchens and astounded each other with unusual creations). And eventually I went for long walks with Teddy Wilson during which we told each other our troubles.

5   My early experiences laid the groundwork for the attitudes I carried into adult life. In a recent discussion with David M. Moss, Ph.D., psychotherapist on the staff of Lutheran General Hospital's Consultation Center in Park Ridge, Illinois, he told me, "The development of healthy friendships grows out of the trust we

learn and experience in childhood. Self-trust and trust of others are learned as early as the first year in life. From then on the presence or absence of trust is relearned and reexperienced in relationships with siblings, peers, and authority figures." I learned from my experience that it is not only possible but also desirable and highly rewarding for women and men to have platonic friendships. Shared interests between a man and woman need not include sex.

6   "The richness of platonic relationships can be enjoyed," says Dr. Moss, "if we draw responsible boundaries in our use of sexuality." However, choosing to have platonic friendships does not necessarily correspond to what may be in the minds of others. Pressures from outside a relationship can be very discomfiting.

7   Is it worth it, then? That depends. It's easier to be what others expect us to be. It would have been easy for me to remain Rehn Peterson's sister and let it go at that. Claiming identity is an effort. But the effort has given me the pleasures of friendship and good memories I will always keep.

A SECOND LOOK

1. According to the author, how is a strong self-identity related to platonic friendship?

2. It is possible to define a term without ever using a dictionary definition. What is Franco's method of defining platonic friendships in paragraph 5? It is also possible to define by giving examples. What examples of platonic friendships does the author mention?

3. Why does the author begin the essay with a personal experience? Point out some of the specific details that make the description of the experience interesting.

IDEAS FOR WRITING

1. Write about a relationship with someone you consider a platonic friend. Begin by choosing the person; then list the interests you have in common. Recall some specific experiences that show these com-

mon interests, and arrange them from earliest to most recent or from least to most important. When you write about this relationship, assume that your readers know what a platonic friendship is but that they have never met the friend you are describing.

2. Have you ever been treated like someone's son, daughter, brother, sister, or friend rather than as an individual? Describe that experience. Remember to use specific details.

SKIING WITH THE GUYS

Catherine Ettlinger

LOOKING FORWARD

When Catherine Ettlinger, managing editor of *Mademoiselle* magazine, goes heli-skiing with a group of advanced skiers, she finds herself the only woman in the company of eleven men, "a macho bunch." She describes how she is able to become "one of the guys" and keep her feminine identity at the same time.

HELP WITH WORDS

careened *(paragraph 1):* tilted

pangs *(paragraph 2):* pains

pervasive *(paragraph 4):* wide-spread

relishing *(paragraph 6):* greatly enjoying

tabloid *(paragraph 6):* a newspaper often featuring sensational stories and headlines

non sequitur *(paragraph 8):* something that does not follow logically

preamble *(paragraph 8):* introductory remarks

veritable *(paragraph 9):* actual

litany *(paragraph 16):* series

epiphany *(paragraph 17):* a sudden revelation

maliciously *(paragraph 17):* cruelly or viciously

prowess *(paragraph 18):* ability

precariously *(paragraph 23):* dangerously

precluded *(paragraph 24):* prevented

traverses *(paragraph 25):* cross-overs

rendered *(paragraph 28):* made

pariah *(paragraph 28):* a misfit or outcast

---

1   The helicopter careened, climbed, dove, floated and hovered until a safe landing was found: the point of a peak that dropped sharply on all four sides, a vertical view down a mountainside in the Canadian Rockies that fell into the sky.

2   We stayed close to put on our skis, and then, following our guide, Ian, one by one so as not to loosen the snow and start a slide, we edged around the shoulder of the peak until we came to the mouth of a wide gully that dropped at a 40-degree angle, one of the steepest pitches I'd ever seen. Just me and 11 guys, strangers in pursuit of the ultimate ski experience. And though I'd done this before (this was my third trip heli-skiing with Canadian Mountain Holidays in the boonies of British Columbia), can-I-keep-up pangs were now gathering in my gut.

3   Two of the guys started down after Ian, then two more, making tracks that slithered away like snakes in the thigh-high April powder. The six others looked to me. This would be my reckoning. I pushed off the lip, catching air (always good for points) and sank into the champagne powder. As I rose to make my first turn I had my rhythm: two, three, four turns, free-falling down the steep from one to another, face shot after face shot of powder dusting my glasses. After two dozen or so turns, the pitch flattened and my tight turns became lovely, long loopy ones. Easing from edge to edge and back again, I pulled up to the others, thinking this was the absolute best that skiing has to offer. Endless expanses of virgin wilderness in every direction. I felt like one of the luckiest people alive.

4   It wasn't easy being a girl among guys out for a pure jock experience. Pervasive in the lodge is a locker-room logic that turns avalanche scares and close-call falls into badges of courage—and any woman into a stereotype who associates powder more with makeup than skiing and who never goes anywhere her blow-dryer can't go.

5   It had taken me two days to get into this group. I was put at first with those who had come for the "Learn to Ski Powder Week"; no questions asked, it went without saying that I couldn't keep up with the big boys. But I was bored until I was moved up to the intermediate level in the afternoon. The next day I was promoted to the advanced group—a macho bunch—and skied with them until high winds forced us back to the lodge just before lunch the next day (the lodges are so isolated, they can be reached only by helicopter in the winter).

6   Deciding not to waste the afternoon indoors, I put on cross-country skis and took off along an old logging road, relishing the majesty of the mountains and the solitude. About an hour out I saw some cat tracks (as in cougar), and the city side of me did an about-face. I headed home to the lodge, visions of gruesome tabloid headlines dancing in my mind. Going along at a pretty good clip I ran into two guys heading out.

7   "Beautiful, isn't it?" I asked.

8   "Great exercise" was one guy's retort—a non sequitur, I thought. That night after dinner the same guy, Reb (yes, that's short for Rebel—he'd already won points for wearing a T-shirt and shell when everyone else was bundled up in down), sat next to me and, without any preamble, asked, "Why aren't you married?" I asked why he was, and left for the far side of the room.

9   I'd encountered the same sort of boldness on my second heli-ski trip: Early in the week three men, veritable strangers, had asked me to spend the night with them. At the time I was insulted. In retrospect I realized the offers were merely an extension of the macho flexing that underscores the whole heli-ski experience—and puts me, as a woman, on the outside.

10   Imagine how I felt, then, when the next morning at breakfast Reb turned up again: "We had a deserter in our group; a guy was called back home for some emergency. Wanna join up?"

11   Like the army? "Is this a joke?" I asked. His was the fastest group of the four.

12   "Nope. We want a woman."

13   "Filling a quota?"

14   "No, seriously, we heard you're a real good skier, and we'd like it very much if you'd join us."

15   In that case (skier first, woman second): "Sure."

16   As my new group waited for the helicopter to pick us up in front of the lodge, Dave, a third-year law student, began a litany

of the dirtiest dirty jokes I'd ever heard. Was this for my benefit, to make me feel uncomfortable? The sinking feeling in the pit of my stomach returned. After we landed the jokes started all over again. Then Howard, a friend of Reb's and one of his three ski buddies from California, stepped to the edge of the ledge to urinate. Ian, our guide that day (the four guides rotate from group to group), warned, "Howard, watch it, you're getting kind of close." We all looked over, worried. Ian added: "Howard, you don't have much to hang on to out there." I was the first to laugh. . . .

17   Suddenly everything was different: I was one of the guys. I could ski, and I could join in the fun too. Then and there I had an epiphany of sorts: Those dirty jokes weren't maliciously intended to make me feel uneasy and unwanted; they were simply part of the experience. Had they not told those jokes on my account, that would indeed have made me an outsider.

18   A funny thing happened after I joined the fraternity: My "prowess" allowed me to be treated like a "princess." Now whoever was the doorman (last in, first out of the helicopter) offered me a hand. Whoever was the tail and carried the reserve pack always asked if I wanted him to carry anything extra. Whoever saw my skis unloaded before I did would hand them to me. I felt protected. In return I was expected to ski hard. Run after run, as we held up our ends of the unspoken bargain, I began to see heli-skiing as the essence of the whole man/woman thing: Men being their most boyish like to treat women (who can cut it) like girls.

19   That first night I joined the group I took extra care dressing for dinner. These guys knew I could ski and laugh at their dirty jokes . . . now it was time to identify myself as pure woman. I purposefully picked my pink shirt (prettier) over my blue one with stars (funkier); leggings (sexier) over jeans (jockier). And I chose black flats, no socks over just socks (sloppy) or sneakers (clunky). My hair, which one guy told me he loved because it was so natural (it was a mess! I'll never understand men!), got moussed and sprayed and scrunched until it was unnaturally full and curly; then I tied on a bow and, from my earlobes, hung pink gemstone hearts that matched my shirt. The result: Coco Chanel Goes Skiing.

20   The group saved me a seat (dinner is family style), and over good food and wine I heard about money-making innovations and miserable marriages, management techniques and dual-career controversies, new restaurants and new reads. By dessert we'd

crossed an emotional line equal to the physical one we'd crossed that day—and created a bond. Little did I know, it would be put to the test the next morning.

21   The daily rotation had given us the first-group-out spot. . . . The company photographer, up for the week to shoot pictures for the new brochure, wanted to join our group because 1) we could make perfect turns and 2) we were first out and would take the first untracked lines down the glacier we were headed for. The problem was that our group had no space, so if he were to join, someone would have to drop back to a less skillful group. I realized that I, having no seniority, would be the "guy" to go.

22   Instead a couple of the guys went to the guide room and said, "We've got a great group, no laggers, and we want to keep it intact." No names, nothing. That was that.

23   The sky broke blue that morning, and the first run out we landed in the crease between two peaks on Conrad Glacier. We skied the wide-open glacier most of the morning, then we chopper-hopped over to a run called Scapula for some skiing through trees. "OK, now we'll see if you can ski the tough stuff." With that, Thierry, our guide that day, started down. We followed him around patches of pines until we reached a precariously steep mountainside hugged by trees so huge they left little ski space between them. "Get partners and stick together," he said. "I'll go down and make the left border; over there several hundred meters is a drop—that's your right border. I'll wait at the bottom." And he was off, yodeling so we could hear the right direction.

24   Just before I felt like the uncoordinated, unpopular third-grade kid who's always last picked for the team, Reb, the best of the bunch, picked me. (Skier's etiquette precluded me from choosing him, because he's better than I and I would slow his run.) "I'll follow you," he said. Okay. Go for it.

25   I took a breath and shoved off. Fast. Hard. Straight down, no traverses. Feel it. Don't think it. Tight. One turn after another, and another. Breathe. Ducking, dodging branches. In the air. Turn again, again, again. Breathe. Faster. He's on my tail. Go, give it all you've got. Now. More. Keep it up. Another turn and another. And then I fell, skis skewed to avoid tumbling into a tree well. He fell too but only to avoid crashing into me. Practically gasping for air, I looked over, a "sorry" on my face. Smiling, he said, "Thanks, that was the best of the week."

26   Though I knew he'd have made the whole run (and knew he

knew it too) if he'd gone with someone else, he meant what he said. It was a great run, maybe not as fast and furious as it might have been, but it was great in another sense: He'd pushed me, I was able to meet the challenge respectably, and he relished that—and seemed to take (more than) equal credit for my performance. It was as though he'd given birth to the skier in me.

27   The harder I skied the better I got, and I felt the others too took pleasure in my progress. Like when Dave coaxed me over a (huge!) jump and I made it. Like when Buck, one of the guides, insisted I carry the reserve pack, knowing I could . . . and I could. Like when Howard said to follow right behind him, no stopping, top to bottom, and I did. Like when I skied too far below the cutoff to the helicopter landing and had to climb up a couple hundred feet in a thigh-deep powder and I did it, and the next runs too, never holding anyone up.

28   And they took equal pleasure in the idea that I was female, that I would wear a pink bow in my hair and hearts in my ears. What had first rendered me a pariah, the notion that I was a city woman whose idea of enjoying the outdoors was to open my window, finally tipped the scale to achieve in the most perfect wilderness a perfect balance between the sexes.

A SECOND LOOK

1. Ettlinger begins with a description of a particular skiing experience. When do you begin to see what her true subject will be? Should she have indicated it earlier? Why or why not?

2. One way in which Ettlinger shows, rather than tells, her readers what happens is by using lively verbs and accurate, interesting adjectives. Pick out several examples.

3. The writer uses at least two levels of language in this essay: fairly formal and very informal. Pick out examples of both. Why do you think she mixes these levels? Do you feel that this technique is effective? Why or why not?

4. How does Ettlinger attack the locker-room prejudice of the other skiers?

5. Ettlinger says she became "one of the guys" while keeping her identity "as pure woman." Do you agree or do you think she went against her own standards of feminine behavior? Explain.

IDEAS FOR WRITING

1. Reread paragraphs 3 and 24. Notice how Ettlinger describes action. Try writing a paragraph or two of your own describing a short period of rapid, intense action such as that of skiing, skating, running, gymnastics, and so forth.

2. Tell of an experience in which you were accepted by a group that formerly had excluded you. Tell your readers exactly what the group was, why it excluded you, and what you did to gain acceptance into it.

3. Marjorie Franco and Catherine Ettlinger both write about platonic friendships, but they differ in their description of how these friendships are formed. In a paragraph or two, summarize the differences in their points of view.

ROPE

Katherine Anne Porter

LOOKING FORWARD

Katherine Anne Porter's short story about the strained relationship between a man and a woman does not directly state a central point. Instead, the reader gradually understands the situation and the two characters by what is said and done in the story. It is important to consider why the characters emphasize particular insults and annoyances.

HELP WITH WORDS

heckle *(paragraph 14):* to annoy with insulting remarks

tyrannize over *(paragraph 14):* to rule cruelly

forlorn *(paragraph 15):* sad

sweltering *(paragraph 21):* extremely hot

melancholiac *(paragraph 22):* someone who suffers from depression

livid *(paragraph 25):* pale

uproarious *(paragraph 28):* extremely funny

wary *(paragraph 35):* cautious

1 On the third day after they moved to the country he came walking back from the village carrying a basket of groceries and a twenty-four-yard coil of rope. She came out to meet him, wiping her hands on her green smock. Her hair was

tumbled, her nose was scarlet with sunburn; he told her that already she looked like a born country woman. His gray flannel shirt stuck to him, his heavy shoes were dusty. She assured him he looked like a rural character in a play.

2   Had he brought the coffee? She had been waiting all day long for coffee. They had forgot it when they ordered at the store the first day.

3   Gosh, no, he hadn't. Lord, now he'd have to go back. Yes, he would if it killed him. He thought, though, he had everything else. She reminded him it was only because he didn't drink coffee himself. If he did he would remember it quick enough. Suppose they ran out of cigarettes? Then she saw the rope. What was that for? Well, he thought it might do to hang clothes on, or something. Naturally she asked him if he thought they were going to run a laundry? They already had a fifty-foot line hanging right before his eyes? Why, hadn't he noticed it, really? It was a blot on the landscape to her.

4   He thought there were a lot of things a rope might come in handy for. She wanted to know what, for instance. He thought a few seconds, but nothing occurred. They could wait and see, couldn't they? You need all sorts of strange odds and ends around a place in the country. She said, yes, that was so; but she thought just at that time when every penny counted, it seemed funny to buy more rope. That was all. She hadn't meant anything else. She hadn't just seen, not at first, why he felt it was necessary.

5   Well, thunder, he had bought it because he wanted to, and that was all there was to it. She thought that was reason enough, and couldn't understand why he hadn't said so, at first. Undoubtedly it would be useful, twenty-four yards of rope, there were hundreds of things, she couldn't think of any at the moment, but it would come in. Of course. As he had said, things always did in the country.

6   But she was a little disappointed about the coffee, and oh, look, look, look at the eggs! Oh, my, they're all running! What had he put on top of them? Hadn't he known eggs mustn't be squeezed? Squeezed, who had squeezed them, he wanted to know. What a silly thing to say. He had simply brought them along in the basket with the other things. If they got broke it was the grocer's fault. He should know better than to put heavy things on top of eggs.

7   She believed it was the rope. That was the heaviest thing in the pack, she saw him plainly when he came in from the road, the rope was a big package on top of everything. He desired the whole wide world to witness that this was not a fact. He had carried the rope in one hand and the basket in the other, and what was the use of her having eyes if that was the best they could do for her?

8   Well, anyhow, she could see one thing plain: no eggs for breakfast. They'd have to scramble them now, for supper. It was too damned bad. She had planned to have steak for supper. No ice, meat wouldn't keep. He wanted to know why she couldn't finish breaking the eggs in a bowl and set them in a cool place.

9   Cool place! if he could find one for her, she'd be glad to set them there. Well, then, it seemed to him they might very well cook the meat at the same time they cooked the eggs and then warm up the meat for tomorrow. The idea simply choked her. Warmed-over meat, when they might as well have had it fresh. Second best and scraps and makeshifts, even to the meat! He rubbed her shoulder a little. It doesn't really matter so much, does it, darling? Sometimes when they were playful, he would rub her shoulder and she would arch and purr. This time she hissed and almost clawed. He was getting ready to say that they could surely manage somehow when she turned on him and said, if he told her they could manage somehow she would certainly slap his face.

10   He swallowed the words red hot, his face burned. He picked up the rope and started to put it on the top shelf. She would not have it on the top shelf, the jars and tins belonged there; positively she would not have the top shelf cluttered up with a lot of rope. She had borne all the clutter she meant to bear in the flat in town, there was space here at least and she meant to keep things in order.

11   Well, in that case, he wanted to know what the hammer and nails were doing up there? And why had she put them there when she knew very well he needed that hammer and those nails upstairs to fix the window sashes? She simply slowed down everything and made double work on the place with her insane habit of changing things around and hiding them.

12   She was sure she begged his pardon, and if she had had any reason to believe he was going to fix the sashes this summer she would have left the hammer and nails right where he put them; in the middle of the bedroom floor where they could step on them in

the dark. And now if he didn't clear the whole mess out of there she would throw them down the well.

13   Oh, all right, all right—could he put them in the closet? Naturally not, there were brooms and mops and dustpans in the closet, and why couldn't he find a place for his rope outside her kitchen? Had he stopped to consider there were seven God-forsaken rooms in the house, and only one kitchen?

14   He wanted to know what of it? And did she realize she was making a complete fool of herself? And what did she take him for, a three-year-old idiot? The whole trouble with her was she needed something weaker than she was to heckle and tyrannize over. He wished to God now they had a couple of children she could take it out on. Maybe he'd get some rest.

15   Her face changed at this, she reminded him he had forgot the coffee and had bought a worthless piece of rope. And when she thought of all the things they actually needed to make the place even decently fit to live in, well, she could cry, that was all. She looked so forlorn, so lost and despairing he couldn't believe it was only a piece of rope that was causing all the racket. What was the matter, for God's sake?

16   Oh, would he please hush and go away, and stay away, if he could, for five minutes? By all means, yes, he would. He'd stay away indefinitely if she wished. Lord, yes, there was nothing he'd like better than to clear out and never come back. She couldn't for the life of her see what was holding him, then. It was a swell time. Here she was, stuck, miles from a railroad, with a half-empty house on her hands, and not a penny in her pocket, and everything on earth to do; it seemed the God-sent moment for him to get out from under. She was surprised he hadn't stayed in town as it was until she had come out and done the work and got things straightened out. It was his usual trick.

17   It appeared to him that this was going a little far. Just a touch out of bounds, if she didn't mind his saying so. Why the hell had he stayed in town the summer before? To do a half-dozen extra jobs to get the money he had sent her. That was it. She knew perfectly well they couldn't have done it otherwise. She had agreed with him at the time. And that was the only time so help him he had ever left her to do anything by herself.

18   Oh, he could tell that to his great-grandmother. She had her notion of what had kept him in town. Considerably more than a notion, if he wanted to know. So, she was going to bring all that up

again, was she? Well, she could just think what she pleased. He was tired of explaining. It may have looked funny but he had simply got hooked in, and what could he do? It was impossible to believe that she was going to take it seriously. Yes, yes, she knew how it was with a man: if he was left by himself a minute, some woman was certain to kidnap him. And naturally he couldn't hurt her feelings by refusing!

19   Well, what was she raving about? Did she forget she had told him those two weeks alone in the country were the happiest she had known for four years? And how long had they been married when she said that? All right, shut up! If she thought that hadn't stuck in his craw.

20   She hadn't meant she was happy because she was away from him. She meant she was happy getting the devilish house nice and ready for him. That was what she had meant, and now look! Bringing up something she had said a year ago simply to justify himself for forgetting her coffee and breaking the eggs and buying a wretched piece of rope they couldn't afford. She really thought it was time to drop the subject, and now she wanted only two things in the world. She wanted him to get that rope from underfoot, and go back to the village and get her coffee, and if he could remember it, he might bring a metal mitt for the skillets, and two more curtain rods, and if there were any rubber gloves in the village, her hands were simply raw, and a bottle of milk of magnesia from the drugstore.

21   He looked out at the dark blue afternoon sweltering on the slopes, and mopped his forehead and sighed heavily and said, if only she could wait a minute for anything, he was going back. He had said so, hadn't he, the very instant they found he had overlooked it?

22   Oh, yes, well . . . run along. She was going to wash windows. The country was so beautiful! She doubted they'd have a moment to enjoy it. He meant to go, but he could not until he had said that if she wasn't such a hopeless melancholiac she might see that this was only for a few days. Couldn't she remember anything pleasant about the other summers? Hadn't they ever had any fun? She hadn't time to talk about it, and now would he please not leave that rope lying around for her to trip on? He picked it up, somehow it had toppled off the table, and walked out with it under his arm.

23   Was he going this minute? He certainly was. She thought so.

Sometimes it seemed to her he had second sight about the precisely perfect moment to leave her ditched. She had meant to put the
mattresses out to sun, if they put them out this minute they
would get at least three hours, he must have heard her say that
morning she meant to put them out. So of course he would walk
off and leave her to it. She supposed he thought the exercise
would do her good.

24   Well, he was merely going to get the coffee. A four-mile walk
for two pounds of coffee was ridiculous, but he was perfectly
willing to do it. The habit was making a wreck of her, but if she
wanted to wreck herself there was nothing he could do about it. If
he thought it was coffee that was making a wreck of her, she
congratulated him: he must have a damned easy conscience.

25   Conscience or no conscience, he didn't see why the mattresses
couldn't very well wait until tomorrow. And anyhow, for God's
sake, were they living in the house, or were they going to let the
house ride them to death? She paled at this, her face grew livid
about the mouth, she looked quite dangerous, and reminded him
that housekeeping was no more her work than it was his: she had
other work to do as well, and when did he think she was going to
find time to do it at this rate?

26   Was she going to start on that again? She knew as well as he
did that his work brought in the regular money, hers was only
occasional, if they depended on what she made—and she might as
well get straight on this question once for all!

27   That was positively not the point. The question was, when both
of them were working on their own time, was there going to be a
division of the housework, or wasn't there? She merely wanted to
know, she had to make her plans. Why, he thought that was all
arranged. It was understood that he was to help. Hadn't he always, in summers?

28   Hadn't he, though? Oh, just hadn't he? And when, and where,
and doing what? Lord, what an uproarious joke!

29   It was such a very uproarious joke that her face turned slightly
purple, and she screamed with laughter. She laughed so hard she
had to sit down, and finally a rush of tears spurted from her eyes
and poured down into the lifted corners of her mouth. He dashed
towards her and dragged her up to her feet and tried to pour water
on her head. The dipper hung by a string on a nail and he broke it
loose. Then he tried to pump water with one hand while she

struggled in the other. So he gave it up and shook her instead.

30 She wrenched away, crying out for him to take his rope and go to hell, she had simply given him up: and ran. He heard her high-heeled bedroom slippers clattering and stumbling on the stairs.

31 He went out around the house and into the lane; he suddenly realized he had a blister on his heel and his shirt felt as if it were on fire. Things broke so suddenly you didn't know where you were. She could work herself into a fury about simply nothing. She was terrible, damn it: not an ounce of reason. You might as well talk to a sieve as that woman when she got going. Damned if he'd spend his life humoring her! Well, what to do now? He would take back the rope and exchange it for something else. Things accumulated, things were mountainous, you couldn't move them or sort them out or get rid of them. They just lay and rotted around. He'd take it back. Hell, why should he? He wanted it. What was it anyhow? A piece of rope. Imagine anybody caring more about a piece of rope than about a man's feelings. What earthly right had she to say a word about it? He remembered all the useless, meaningless things she bought for herself: Why? because I wanted it, that's why! He stopped and selected a large stone by the road. He would put the rope behind it. He would put it in the tool-box when he got back. He'd heard enough about it to last him a life-time.

32 When he came back she was leaning against the post box beside the road waiting. It was pretty late, the smell of broiled steak floated nose high in the cooling air. Her face was young and smooth and fresh-looking. Her unmanageable funny black hair was all on end. She waved to him from a distance, and he speeded up. She called out that supper was ready and waiting, was he starved?

33 You bet he was starved. Here was the coffee. He waved it at her. She looked at his other hand. What was that he had there?

34 Well, it was the rope again. He stopped short. He had meant to exchange it but forgot. She wanted to know why he should exchange it, if it was something he really wanted. Wasn't the air sweet now, and wasn't it fine to be here?

35 She walked beside him with one hand hooked into his leather belt. She pulled and jostled him a little as he walked, and leaned against him. He put his arm clear around her and patted her

stomach. They exchanged wary smiles. Coffee, coffee for the Oot-sum-Wootsums! He felt as if he were bringing her a beautiful present.

36   He was a love, she firmly believed, and if she had had her coffee in the morning, she wouldn't have behaved so funny. . . . There was a whippoorwill still coming back, imagine, clear out of season, sitting in the crab-apple tree calling all by himself. Maybe his girl stood him up. Maybe she did. She hoped to hear him once more, she loved whippoorwills. . . . He knew how she was, didn't he?

37   Sure, he knew how she was.

A SECOND LOOK

1. State clearly the situation that exists at the beginning of the story. Where are the characters? Why are they there? What are their circumstances?

2. In several instances it seems that the characters' angry statements suggest more than they actually say. For example, in paragraphs 8 and 9 the woman complains because there is no ice or cool place to keep food from spoiling. Even the thought of warmed-over meat chokes her. But rather than talking about eggs and steak, she seems to be complaining about their lifestyle in the country. She obviously feels she deserves more or better. Look at the insult in paragraph 14 and the woman's response in paragraph 15. What do the words suggest beyond what they actually say? Draw similar conclusions from paragraph 18, paragraphs 25 and 26, and paragraph 34.

3. State the main idea of the story. Make sure that you focus on the larger problems in the couple's relationship.

4. The argument seems to be over by the end of the story. Are you convinced by their loving words that their fighting is over? Why or why not?

5. Imagine for a moment that you are the man in the story. What complaints would you have about the woman? Change roles and state the woman's side of the argument. Who is mostly to blame in this situation?

IDEAS FOR WRITING

Tell about a situation in which you were angry with someone and felt that he or she was to blame for the problem. Make some notes before you start to write. List all the details you remember about the episode. Recall especially those that will help your reader understand why you were angry.

As you write your list, try to recall how you felt during the episode. Porter says of the man in "Rope": ". . . his face burned," and ". . . his shirt felt as if it were on fire." Look for ways of expressing what your anger felt like.

Review your list and select those words and phrases that seem particularly vivid or accurate. Use these as you begin to write the description of the episode.

WOMEN WASTED

Jennifer Bitner

LOOKING FORWARD

In this student essay, Jennifer Bitner considers the differences among three generations of women. As she looks at her grandmother, her mother, and herself, she wonders whether the two older women ever felt as she does now.

HELP WITH WORDS

aspirations *(paragraph 4):* wishes, ambitions

immersed *(paragraph 5):* totally involved

---

1   She sits in the living room of my aunt's house surrounded by blurry colors and shapeless movements. Noises come to her through layers of cotton. Ninety-five years have made her crumple and sag. She is a dying old creature.

2   She seems so happy; she smiles and hugs me to her softly. Her glassy eyes search out the blur that is my face and kiss it, missing my mouth, but giving me a wonderful nose kiss. In a way, her warm presence is comforting to me, but it also frightens me.

3   What is there to connect me to this strange old woman who lives strongly in the past, while I am searching for a future? What could I possibly share with someone so old, so near death? Was there any fun, any joy, in her life spent serving husband and children? When I look at an old picture of my grandmother, strange feelings come over me. I have a beautiful picture showing

her at about my age. Her hair is pulled back in a soft bun, and her eyes are warm and proud. Her mouth is curved in my smile. I look like the woman in the picture, yet she is so far from the dying woman in the E-Z Boy rocker, and both are far from me.

4 If I could talk to the girl in the picture, would she be like me? Did she have many dreams? I am sure she dreamed of more than this. She must have had aspirations beyond motherhood, though she probably was not nearly as ambitious as I am. She was a woman at a time when woman meant wife and mother.

5 Fear hits me, the same fear I feel when I watch my mother clean the house or make my father's dinner. She is so immersed in these simple tasks, as if in a trance. I love these women, but my body and mind cry out that I will not be like them. I cannot confine myself to mindless tasks and unending service.

6 These women missed so much playing the role of wife and mother. Neither went to college; both stayed home and cared for children and house. They do not know what they missed out on—do they?

7 Does my mother ever get a vague feeling of distress? At night does she think, "Who am I and what have I done for myself? Where was *my* life in this tangle of years?"

8 Grandmother is too old to cry for. She smiles and in her semi-senility is content, but I cry for my mother. The only job she ever held was as a secretary. Her life was spent in marriage and raising children. I know she gets depressed sometimes. Does she realize she has a mind she is wasting?

9 I cry for my mother, and her mother, and for all of the women who have been wasted. Minds, wonderful minds, wasted on dishes and hours of boredom. All of these things I think as I hug this old woman and hear the chatter of my mother in the next room gossiping.

A SECOND LOOK

1. One of the writer's strengths is her ability to give us clear pictures of people in just a few sentences. What details help us see what kind of women her grandmother and her mother are?

2. In paragraphs 2 and 5, Bitner says she feels fear. What is she afraid of? Why doesn't she express her fear more directly?

3. What is the writer's attitude toward the traditional role of women? What details indicate this attitude? Do you agree or disagree with her? Why?

IDEAS FOR WRITING

1. Perhaps you disagree with Jennifer Bitner's view of the role of wife and mother. (Review your answer to "A Second Look," question 3.) If so, write a paper in which you give the advantages of a woman's remaining in the home to care for her family. You may wish to list both negative and positive aspects, but your main idea will be that there are still good reasons for a woman to choose the traditional role of wife and mother. If your instructor wishes, you could first discuss the topic in small groups in class.

2. If you are a woman reading this essay, you may feel as Bitner does when you compare yourself to your mother, aunts, grandmothers, or other older women in your family. If so, write a paper in which you describe their attitudes and yours, explaining the differences between them. You might consider Bitner's question: "They do not know what they missed out on—do they?"

3. If you are a man reading this essay, you may be able to look at your father and grandfather and view the situation from their side. Do men of earlier generations have regrets—too much time spent at work and not enough at home, too many years when their children grew up almost without their noticing, too little time spent with their wives? If you think your life will be different, then describe what those differences will be. In other words, write about Jennifer Bitner's topic from a male point of view.

MAKING CONNECTIONS

Marjorie Franco writes that one difficulty in forming relationships is pressure from outside those relationships. We are influenced by what others think. As Franco puts it. "It's easier to be what others expect us to be."

In the four selections in this unit, some of the women conform to what others expect of them and some do not. Which women belong in which category? Considering what happens to these women, do you agree that "it's easier to be what others expect us to be"? Is the situation different for men?

FRONTIERS

LIFE AFTER DEATH: THE GROWING EVIDENCE

Mary Ann O'Roark

LOOKING FORWARD

This essay presents a survey of the evidence that has been collected on a controversial topic: life after death. The author does not try to persuade the reader to accept the evidence as truth, but she does suggest that it not be dismissed lightly. The examples used in the essay may show that death is a frontier that has already been crossed by some who returned to tell about it.

HELP WITH WORDS

vibrant *(paragraph 2):* full of energy

skepticism *(paragraph 6):* doubt

authenticity *(paragraph 6):* genuineness

anecdotal *(paragraph 7):* like a story

compelling *(paragraph 8):* having a powerful effect

document *(paragraph 8):* give evidence

verifiable *(paragraph 8):* able to be proved

rigorous *(paragraph 8):* strict

scrutiny *(paragraph 8):* an examination

lucid *(paragraph 9):* clear

predispose *(paragraph 9):* determine in advance

euphoria *(paragraph 9):* a feeling of well being or elation

lustrous *(paragraph 10):* shining

fabrications *(paragraph 11):* made-up stories

grapple *(paragraph 13):* struggle

prudent *(paragraph 14):* careful in providing for the future

eventuality *(paragraph 14):* a possible occurrence

---

1   Fifty-five-year-old Virginia Falce describes herself as "a quiet, old-fashioned person, as normal as they come." Her laugh is warm and lively, her manner reassuring. She remembers what happened to her "as clear as if it were yesterday." During an otherwise routine tonsillectomy, her heart stopped. Hospital records show that for three minutes doctors performed open-heart surgery, cutting open her chest to massage her heart by hand.

2   She describes her experience in a vibrant, steady voice. "All of a sudden I was awake, and I was rising through a white mist. Then it was all dark. I wasn't frightened—a little curious, I guess, just like a kid. I wondered, Hmmmm, what's happening? But I didn't feel funny that nothing was underneath me and that I didn't have a body any more. I felt quite at home, really. It wasn't the world I was used to, but it didn't bother me at all. I know it sounds strange, but it's true. Then I felt this sense of absolute love and peace embracing me, pulling me from somewhere. I looked over and I could see that it was coming from this glowing circle of light. I wasn't the kind of person who went to church—I didn't believe in all that stuff. But I looked over and I knew this light was God, and it was such love and joy that I wanted to go to it forever. Oh, I know what drugs or anesthesia make you feel like, and this wasn't like that at all. What I'm telling wasn't *like* it was real—it *was* real.

3   "Then somehow the thought came into my mind that I ought to go back, that I had two children. But I said, No, I don't want to go back. And I loved my life, I loved my children! But this presence of love was so powerful—pure love without all of the earthly attachments of guilt and pain and anxiety—it was all I wanted. But then out of pure logic I decided I had a job to do and I had to return.

4   "The next thing I remember was the nurse standing over my bed saying, 'I thought we'd lost you,' and people coming in and asking me what it was like to die.

5   "The funny thing is that I was always so afraid of death. And now here I was in the hospital with a heart so bad the doctors thought it might stop again at any minute, and I was not one bit afraid. In the years since, I've had to be careful, and I had a heart attack recently, and I was as calm as anything. I love life and helping people, but don't mind the idea of death a bit. I don't have a moment's fear about what's waiting for me."

6   Stories like this are moving, but they are not new. They have been quietly heard here and there for years. What is new is a readiness on the part of physicians and scholars in this country to listen to them seriously and study them as legitimate data worthy of professional research. Today scientists who once might have regarded these accounts with skepticism are becoming increasingly convinced of their authenticity and value.

7   In her book *On Death and Dying* (1969) Dr. Elisabeth Kübler-Ross, a psychiatrist, told of the many cases she had encountered in which people close to death reported "heavenly" experiences. And in 1975 Dr. Raymond A. Moody published *Life After Life*, in which he reported in anecdotal fashion over a hundred cases he had encountered as a physician.

8   Both sets of experiences had startling similarities: People close to death told of feelings of acceptance and peace and the presence of welcoming loved ones. But as compelling as Dr. Kübler-Ross's stories are, she did not document them by publishing verifiable medical records. And Raymond Moody himself pointed out that his own cases, although completely authentic, had not been researched and recorded according to rigorous scientific and medical procedures. The question was, would such stories stand up under closer scrutiny?

9   Both baffled and fascinated by these accounts, University of Connecticut psychologist and professor Kenneth Ring set out to find an entirely new group of people who had come close to death. In a thoughtful and lucid book, *Life at Death: A Scientific Investigation of the Near-Death Experience*, he tells of over a hundred cases that he researched in detail in Connecticut and Maine. Ring and his associates collected and verified as much information about these people as possible. Did they share the same religious expectations or psychological histories that might predispose

them to such "visions"? Could their states of euphoria be traced to drugs—or be the result of intense anxiety? And what exactly were their experiences? Was there anything to support Moody and Kübler-Ross in their findings?

10   In the course of his research, Ring found that his subjects—men and women of a wide range of age, education, background and temperament—all spoke of what he came to call a "core experience," which occurred when they were close to death or "clinically dead." They told of floating up and away from their bodies, of communicating with loved ones who were already dead, of gliding down a dark tunnel toward a lustrous light, of reaching a place they sensed was a threshold but from which they were drawn back, sometimes by a sense of responsibility toward others. Although there were variations in the accounts—not everyone told of the happenings in the same sequence, or experienced all of them—the feeling was always the same: There was a sense of great comfort and even bliss in which the person longed to remain and whose positive intensity was carried back to affect the rest of that person's life in the "earthly" world. Regardless of what their attitudes had been before—and their religious beliefs varied widely—these people were convinced that they had been in the presence of some supreme and loving power and had been given a glimpse of a life yet to come. . . .

11   "No one who meets these people and hears their stories can come away without being profoundly stirred—emotionally, intellectually, spiritually," Ring says. "I'm convinced that these are absolutely authentic experiences. They're not dreams, they're not fabrications—they're meaningful experiences that cannot be dismissed or disregarded. They're real in their effect on human conduct, which to me is the important point."

12   Over the past ten years, Dr. Ian Stevenson, Carlson professor of psychiatry at the University of Virginia Medical Center, has studied many cases of near-death experiences; his reports have been published by the *Journal of Nervous and Mental Disease* and the *American Journal of Psychiatry*, as well as by university presses.

13   "People sometimes ask me if I believe in rebirth and survival after death," he says. "But that's the wrong kind of question. People shouldn't ask what I believe, they should ask what they believe. Our job is not to convince or convert anybody, but simply to chart the evidence and present it in a form that people can

judge and grapple with for themselves. It's possible that researchers will one day decide that life after death isn't the best explanation for the evidence we have—but it's just as possible that they will decide it is. It's a leap of faith, of course. But I think all scientific advances involve a leap of faith."

14   Personally, Dr. Stevenson speaks for many of those who have closely observed this phenomenon when he says that "there is increasing evidence that we do live after death. I think it prudent to prepare for the eventuality."

A SECOND LOOK

1. Does O'Roark's report of the research on near-death experiences seem generally unbiased? Give reasons for your answer.

2. Why does O'Roark use one complete paragraph (paragraph 12) to explain who Ian Stevenson is and where his reports have been published?

3. Why have scientists begun to take near-death stories more seriously?

4. Kenneth Ring, after completing much research, said that the near-death experiences were "real in their effect on human conduct. . . ." Explain what he meant.

5. After reading this article, what conclusions do you draw about near-death experiences?

IDEAS FOR WRITING

Choose any current topic that interests you and that is written about in today's magazines and newspapers. Read several articles on this topic. If you do not buy many magazines or newspapers, use the library. If you know someone who is knowledgeable about your subject, you may even interview him or her. When you feel you have enough information—using what you already know about the topic and what you have discovered from your reading and discussion—write a short report giving your readers the basic facts about your topic. Your essay will certainly not be as long as Mary Ann O'Roark's, but like her you should use what you have learned to add weight and interest to what you are writing.

You do not have to footnote what you quote, but you should give credit to your sources. Suppose you are writing about an important court case. The following examples show how you can use material from your reading or interviews:

1. John Smith, writing in *The New York Times*, stated that the Supreme Court's decision in the Shaw case was "one of the most important legal decisions of the last twenty-five years."

2. A week after the Supreme Court announced its decision in the Shaw case, *Newsweek* reported that at least a dozen men now awaiting execution were preparing new appeals, believing that the Shaw ruling would affect them also.

3. Jane Doe, an attorney with years of experience in criminal cases of this type, says that the Shaw decision may "open a floodgate. There may be a wave of appeals that will keep the courts busy for the next ten years." Ms. Doe further believes that the Court's ruling will probably have "a very negative effect" on police departments in the nation's larger cities.

OUR BRAIN'S SUCCESSOR

Robert Jastrow

LOOKING FORWARD

Robert Jastrow is a geologist, astronomer, and physicist who teaches at both Columbia University and Dartmouth College. In this look at the future, Professor Jastrow predicts that a new form of intelligence greater than humanity's will evolve. The human brain will soon be inferior to the artificial intelligence of super-computers.

HELP WITH WORDS

snippet *(paragraph 1):* a small piece

parse *(paragraph 2):* analyze the parts of a sentence, such as subject, verb, direct object, and so forth

competent *(paragraph 2):* adequate

inexhaustible *(paragraph 2):* without limit

prospect *(paragraph 4):* view of something to come

jargon *(paragraph 5):* a specialized or technical language

mammoth *(paragraph 7):* huge

subordinate *(paragraph 7):* inferior to another

enhance *(paragraph 10):* make greater or better

facet *(paragraph 10):* a part

1　　T he following snippet of unrehearsed dialogue took place a few years ago between a computer and a human subject:

Subject: Men are all alike.
Computer: IN WHAT WAY
Subject: They're always bugging me about something or other.
Computer: CAN YOU THINK OF A SPECIFIC EXAMPLE
Subject: Well, my boyfriend made me come here.
Computer: YOUR BOYFRIEND MADE YOU COME HERE
Subject: He says I'm depressed much of the time.
Computer: I AM SORRY TO HEAR YOU ARE DEPRESSED

2　　Computers programmed to parse sentences and carry out natural conversations are little more than parlor games, but they demonstrate an eye-opening level of artificial intelligence to anyone who thinks these devices are merely fast adding machines. During the past ten years, machines have taken over a large fraction of clerical jobs in the United States, such as accounting and inventory control; computers fill customer orders and manage airline reservations; and they are beginning to move up into higher levels of management, to make competent decisions on security investments and marketing strategies. Computers also make excellent teachers. They can give personal attention to hundreds of students at a time; their patience is inexhaustible; they are rarely in a hurry to get back to scholarly research; and they are never sarcastic.

3　　If these trends continue, many jobs in businesses and schools will be filled by computer brains that talk, listen and remember everything. They will be there because they cost less to keep in repair than human brains, they aren't unionized, and they never get tired.

4　　Most people find this prospect depressing, but even more unsettling developments are in the works. The latest trends in computer evolution suggest that the inroads of the intelligent machine will not stop, even at fairly high-level jobs. For anyone who believes in the permanent superiority of man over the machine, these trends are alarming.

5　　Since the birth of the modern computer in the 1950s, computers have increased in power and capability by a factor of ten every seven years; seven years is a generation in computer evolution, in the jargon of computer scientists. The first generation of computers was a billion times clumsier and less efficient than the human brain. Today, midway between the fourth and fifth generations, electronic brains are only ten thousand times clumsier than the human brain. The gap has been narrowed. Around 1995, in the seventh computer generation, the gap will be closed entirely.

6   And theoretical physics indicates no early limits to further computer growth: Computers, unlike the human brain, do not have to pass through a birth canal.

7   As these nonbiological intelligences increase in size and capacity, there will be people around to teach them everything they know. One sees a vision of mammoth brains in the next century, which have soaked up the wisdom of the human race and gone on from there. If this forecast is accurate, man is doomed to a subordinate status on his own planet.

8   The story is an old one on the Earth: In the struggle for survival, bigger brains are better. One hundred million years ago, when the brainy little mammal coexisted with the less intelligent dinosaurs, the mammal survived and the dinosaur vanished. It appears that in the next chapter of this unfolding story fate has cast man in the role of the dinosaur.

9   What can be done? The answer is obvious: Pull the plug.

10   That may not be so easy. Computers enhance the productivity of human labor; they create wealth and the leisure to enjoy it; they have ushered in the Golden Age. In fifteen or twenty years, the brightest and the best of computer brains will be advising top-level management on every facet of the nation's existence: the economy, transportation, security, medicine, communications. . . . If someone pulled the plug, chaos would result. The poor fellow would be lynched. There is no turning back anymore. . . .

A SECOND LOOK

1. What is surprising or unexpected about the dialogue between the human being and the computer in paragraph 1?

2. Why does Jastrow believe that computer intelligence will grow faster than human intelligence?

3. Since computers are created by people, why can't we control their development?

IDEAS FOR WRITING

1. In paragraph 2, Jastrow states that "computers make excellent teachers." Have you ever been taught by a computer? If so, compare a human being and a machine as teachers. First, show how a typical human instructor teaches a lesson and how he or she interacts with students. Then show how a computer does the same job. (Remember to provide a link to help your readers know when you change subjects—from human teacher to computer teacher.) You may assume that many of your readers have not had instruction by computer, so explain clearly what it is like. If you wish to explain which kind of teaching you prefer, you may.

2. Researchers are now experimenting with computers as counselors. You may someday be able to give a computer a description of a personal problem; the computer will then analyze it and print out possible solutions in order of their effectiveness. Would you feel comfortable explaining your problems to a computer and getting advice from it? What would be the advantages and disadvantages? Write a short paper explaining your feelings about going to a computer-counselor.

3. Imagine that you are sitting at the console of the computer-counselor described in 2. You are going to input a personal problem in one or two paragraphs. Remember that the computer cannot help by looking concerned and understanding or by nodding its head and saying, "Yes, I see; well, that's too bad." It is entirely up to you to state your problem briefly, clearly, and completely.

THE ANSWER

Fredric Brown

LOOKING FORWARD

In this science fiction story, Fredric Brown creates both suspense and surprise. As you read, notice what details Brown includes so that the reader is quickly able to imagine the time and setting of the story.

HELP WITH WORDS

ceremoniously *(paragraph 1):* formally, very properly

sub-ether *(paragraph 1):* the lower atmosphere

bore *(paragraph 1):* carried

cybernetics machine *(paragraph 2):* an electronic computer

1　**D**war Ev ceremoniously soldered the final connection with gold. The eyes of a dozen television cameras watched him and the sub-ether bore throughout the universe a dozen pictures of what he was doing.

2　He straightened and nodded to Dwar Reyn, then moved to a position beside the switch that would complete the contact when he threw it. The switch that would connect, all at once, all of the monster computing machines of all the populated planets in the universe—96 billion planets—into the supercircuit that would connect them all into one super-calculator, one cybernetics machine that would combine all of the knowledge of the galaxies.

3   Dwar Reyn spoke briefly to the watching and listening trillions. Then after a moment's silence he said, "Now, Dwar Ev."

4   Dwar Ev threw the switch. There was a mighty hum, the surge of power from 96 billion planets. Lights flashed and quieted along the miles-long panel.

5   Dwar Ev stepped back and drew a deep breath. "The honor of asking the first question is yours, Dwar Reyn."

6   "Thank you," said Dwar Reyn. "It shall be a question which no single cybernetics machine has been able to answer."

7   He turned to face the machine. "Is there a God?"

8   The mighty voice answered without hesitation, without the clicking of a single relay.

9   "Yes, *now* there is a God."

10   Sudden fear flashed on the face of Dwar Ev. He leaped to grab the switch.

11   A bolt of lightning from the cloudless sky struck him down and fused the switch shut.

A SECOND LOOK

1. Pick out several details in the first paragraph that suggest that this event is a special occasion.

2. When and where does this event take place? Explain your answer.

3. Why does Dwar Reyn ask the machine if there is a God?

4. What questions does the story raise about man's technological ambitions?

IDEAS FOR WRITING

Imagine that you are in the television audience watching the ceremony described in "The Answer." Describe in two or three paragraphs what happens next. What might the machine-god do or say as it takes over? Assume that your reader is already familiar with events up to the bolt of lightning.

THE HUNGER TO COME

John Laffin

LOOKING FORWARD

In the last chapter of *The Hunger to Come*, John Laffin, who has long been concerned with basic environmental problems such as land management and food production, points out another frontier. After seeing the misery and death caused by world hunger, Laffin believes that if we cannot meet the challenge of this frontier, we may not survive to meet any other.

HELP WITH WORDS

obtrude *(paragraph 2):* intrude; push in where not wanted

FAO *(paragraph 2):* the Food and Agriculture Organization, an agency of the United Nations

magnitude *(paragraph 3):* great size

henceforth *(paragraph 3):* from this time forward

assault *(paragraph 3):* an attack

systematized *(paragraph 4):* put into an orderly plan

George Orwell and Aldous Huxley *(paragraph 4):* British authors whose novels *1984* (Orwell) and *Brave New World* (Huxley) show a future in which life will be controlled by central governments

acute *(paragraph 5):* brief but severe

chronic *(paragraph 5):* continuing over a period of time

reluctantly *(paragraph 7):* with hesitation

prospect *(paragraph 10):* a mental view of something to come

---

1   Mankind has now reached a strange position: Science can save a child's life much more readily than it can ensure that the child will be fed for life. Again, science is making great leaps into space but apparently cannot realize that there is no escape in space for mankind. Other planets cannot support our type of life, nor can we hope to bring food back from them.

2   Nobody can make a truly accurate prediction about the food future, because food does not depend merely on farming. Economic, political, social and cultural influences all obtrude. However, the FAO is confident that humanity need not be starved out of existence, though it does not go so far as to say that this will not happen.

3   The trouble is that all the activity aimed at fighting the problem is not nearly enough. Well-fed countries and people simply do not realize the magnitude of the crisis. They are acting as if by contributing their 2 million pounds or two pounds to a relief organization the mildly distressing situation will go away. But we are facing no passing crisis; we must accept the situation as a fact of life as much with us now and henceforth as is the nuclear bomb. We should do all we can now, while we look at the future imaginatively and with vision, planning an even grander—much grander—assault on the hunger front. . . .

4   There are great dangers in all this planning, international cooperation and systematized approach to food and population. The main one is that of the human race being ruled by social engineers in an internationally planned economy, with all its frightening visions as foreseen by George Orwell and Aldous Huxley. Is this fate preferable to mass starvation? Should you, personally, happen to be hungry, your answer will be definite enough.

5   Let us be under no illusions about the situation. It is vast and complex, and it is with us now, in acute and in chronic form. It is no longer a matter of the life of individuals being in jeopardy, but the safety of the human race.

6   Meanwhile, every hour of every day the human tragedies multiply. They are happening in Brazil and Venezuela, India and Pakistan, Mauritius and Malaya—for hunger knows no frontiers. . . .

7   I was in the hills [of Lebanon] one day and found behind a rock not far from the road a newly born baby, wrapped in a shawl of sacking. Clearly the baby had not been born at the spot, but had been carried there. I assumed that it had been kidnapped and abandoned, probably out of spite. Such things do happen. I took the baby back to Beirut and asked an Arab friend to help me find the mother. Reluctantly, he agreed and after a two-day search and a lot of trouble we located the mother—a woman of about twenty-six living in the Beirut slum.

8   My satisfaction as I carried the infant into the tin hut was deflated by the dull look the woman gave me as she took the child. She just sat there, lifeless, cold, but said something as we left.

9   Outside in the sunshine I asked my friend what the woman said. He gave me a queer look. "She said, 'Why didn't you let him die in peace? He will now only die in hunger pains.'"

10   It is not likely that I could ever forget this incident, but I remembered it particularly when I travelled with a young Indian government doctor to a village north of Calcutta. He was on his way to treat a woman reported as seriously injured; this was one of the few reports of illness that did get through and the woman was one of the relatively few patients the doctor had time to see. She was seriously injured all right, opened up across the abdomen by something sharp and jagged. Further examination disclosed internal injuries as well. The woman, a widow aged about thirty and mother of ten children, eight of them living, died in her hut. She was pregnant and her wounds were the result of a frantic attempt to bring about an abortion. "It must have been just too much," the doctor said. "Her husband died of disease a few months ago. Two of her kids have already died from hunger, the other eight are starving and she couldn't face the prospect of another mouth to feed."

11   "What will happen to the family now?" I asked.

12   The doctor shrugged. "I expect they'll starve." And half a minute later he said, "I hope we can get back to town in time for dinner."

A SECOND LOOK

1. Why does Laffin use the examples of the Lebanese and Indian women at the end rather than the beginning of his chapter?

2. Why is the second example especially effective?

3. In Laffin's view, what are the major causes of the food crisis?

4. Laffin says that we must solve the food problem for "the safety of the human race." Obviously the entire human race will not starve, so what is the danger to mankind?

IDEAS FOR WRITING

A congressional committee is meeting to make decisions about defense spending. You are going to appear before that committee and read a statement supporting the view that part of the money could better be spent on food production than on new weapons. What would you say? Write down several points to support your position, then arrange them in order from least important to most important or from least persuasive to most persuasive. Write the essay as if you were going to read it before the congressional committee.

POWER FROM THE SKY

Joseph Knapka

LOOKING FORWARD

We often assume that growth on Earth is limited by our dwindling resources and that growth beyond our planet is limited by insufficient money and technology. In this student research paper, Joseph Knapka challenges these assumptions and argues that we can cross these frontiers too.

HELP WITH WORDS

biosphere *(paragraph 1):* that area of the Earth's land, water, and atmosphere that can support life

simulation *(paragraph 2):* model

interstellar *(paragraph 5):* among the stars

finite *(paragraph 5):* limited

photovoltaic cells *(paragraph 6):* units that can produce electricity when exposed to light

array *(paragraph 7):* an orderly arrangement

contemplated *(paragraph 7):* considered

alleviate *(paragraph 10):* reduce, lessen

1   T here exists in the world today a school of thought which holds that the resources of man are limited to the resources of the planet on which he evolved—that there is no more living space, energy, or food available to us other than that which we find within the biosphere of Planet Earth. Much of the foundation for this sort of thinking can be found in a slim volume called *The Limits to Growth*, published by a group called the Club of Rome (Heppenheimer, *Future*, 204).

2   The Club of Rome conducted a study in 1971 that, on the surface, seems to support this line of thought. They designed and executed a computerized simulation of the world's economy, taking into account such variables as pollution, population growth, available energy, food, and standard of living. The results of the simulation showed that the collapse of human civilization worldwide was due within the century (205).

3   However, the model used for the study neglected some very important relationships. Possibly the best criticism came from Robert Boyd, of the University of California. A year after the *Limits* model was run, Boyd designed a new version. Starting with the same basic model, he added one more variable: technology. He wrote equations which simulated the assumptions that growth of technology could hold resource availability steady, increase standard of living (and hence indirectly decrease population growth[1]), and/or increase the output of agricultural land. His model provided a much more hopeful viewpoint, predicting a leveling-off of population growth, and a worldwide increase in standard of living, well into the next century (Heppenheimer 205).[2]

4   But the question remains: are Boyd's assumptions necessarily any more correct than the Club of Rome's were? There is evidence that, if people act rationally, the answer is definitely "yes."

5   Consider, for a moment, the sun. With sufficient energy, and means to control it, practically anything can be accomplished, from food synthesis to interstellar flight. Stars are the universe's ultimate energy source, and the human race has a prime specimen right next door. Of course, all energy used today comes from the sun, but only indirectly. Fossil fuels, for instance, are the result of sun-nourished matter being compressed in the crust of the planet. However, fossil fuels are finite resources, and that is one area in which the *Limits to Growth* assumption holds com-

pletely true. Sun and Earth cannot replace our fossil fuels as fast as we use them up. The sun itself, however, being much longer-lived, is almost unlimited in the amount of energy it produces. All we need to do to take advantage of that is to figure out a way of utilizing the sun's energy more directly.

6   Not surprisingly, ways have been thought of to do this. Solar energy has been fairly popular as a home-heating scheme, and photovoltaic cells, or photocells, can be used to convert sunlight directly into electricity. However, these schemes have two problems: the atmosphere, and the planet it surrounds. Cloudless days are rare in most parts of the world, and in any case the Earth's own shadow limits daylight time to a bare 50% of each 24-hour period.

7   The obvious solution to these problems is to put the photocell array above the atmosphere, which is exactly what is being contemplated. Furthermore, since the zero-gravity orbital environment imposes much less stress on large structures than does the Earth's surface gravity, these photocell arrays can be built on a very large scale—conceivably, one array could have a surface area of hundreds of square kilometers. The array would catch sunlight, convert it to electricity, and beam it to ground stations via microwave transmissions. In tests microwave power transmission has efficiency factors of over 70% (Heppenheimer, *Colonies,* 223). The concept of these solar power satellites (SPS) has been around since 1968, and today we have the technology to make it practical (Heppenheimer, *Suns,* 83).

8   The price tag is actually fairly modest when one considers that, after the initial investment is paid off, the energy obtained is essentially free. The most promising estimate was a bid by Boeing Corporation, which claimed that it could have a power satellite operational within a decade, at a total expenditure of under $300 billion. Additional satellites would be much cheaper, since the major investments, primarily the satellite construction station, would already be complete (Heppenheimer, *Colonies,* 147).

9   A single power satellite would have a solar reception area of perhaps ten square kilometers. If the density of solar energy at the Earth's orbit is one watt per square meter, and the photocells convert the solar energy to electricity with 80% efficiency, and the power transmission beam transmits the energy down to the

surface with 70% efficiency, then the total energy obtained would be approximately 6,000,000 × .80 × .70 watts, or 3.36 megawatts. This is approximately enough energy to maintain Manhattan Island's electrical supply on a constant basis.

10   The beauty of the system is that the work force would not need to be large—perhaps five hundred to build the first satellite, although the number would get larger immediately, since it would be necessary to mine the moon and asteroid belts for raw materials. When the population began to expand into space in earnest, huge space stations called O'Niell colonies would be built—essentially self-contained worlds, complete with hills, streams, and cities. They would serve to alleviate much of the population pressure of the homeworld, since a large O'Niell colony could house millions of people. Again, we have the technology today, although not the budget, to build such structures.[3] However, the power satellites would provide us with the financial base needed to colonize space, since we could sell energy to other nations—and man's expansion to the stars could begin.

Notes

[1]When the standard of living of a population rises, its growth rate tends to decrease. This effect causes a decrease in unemployment because of the smaller available work force. These effects were mentioned in *Toward Distant Suns*, but Heppenheimer does not document this information.

[2]This paragraph is summarized from various sections of several of Heppenheimer's works.

[3]This paragraph is summarized from several chapters of Gerard K. O'Niell's *The High Frontier*.

Works Cited

Heppenheimer, T. A. *Colonies in Space.* Harrisburg: Stackpole, 1976.
———. *The Real Future.* New York: Doubleday, 1983.
———. *Toward Distant Suns.* Harrisburg: Stackpole, 1979.
O'Niell, Gerard K. *The High Frontier.* New York: Doubleday, 1982.

A SECOND LOOK

1. In paragraphs 1 and 2, Knapka states an idea with which the rest of his paper disagrees. How does he signal the beginning of his counter-argument in paragraph 3? How does he continue his argument in paragraphs 4 and 5?

2. How are the arguments about increasing energy sources and colonizing space related?

3. Who are the authorities Knapka cites for his support and what do we know about them? How does Knapka's use of authorities differ from that of Mary Ann O'Roark in "Life after Death?" Which method do you think is more effective?

IDEAS FOR WRITING

1. In paragraph 10, Knapka mentions O'Niell colonies, described as "essentially self-contained worlds, complete with hills, streams, and cities . . . [which] could house millions of people." Imagine what life in such a colony would be like. What would be the advantages and disadvantages of living there? What would the inhabitants likely miss most when they moved from Earth? In several paragraphs, describe how you think life in an O'Niell colony would be lived and explain why you would or would not like to try living there.

2. Your instructor may wish you to write a short library paper in which you support your ideas with the ideas of others, just as Joseph Knapka does in "Power from the Sky." If so, pick a subject about which you can easily find material in the library. A few suggestions are: the effects of TV violence, banning books in public schools, mandatory seat belt laws, vitamin therapy for the common cold, and mandatory drug testing for athletes. Your instructor may suggest other topics.

   When you have picked a topic, check the library for information on it. Try to find several books, articles, or newspaper stories stating different points of view. Combine this material with your own ideas as Knapka did in his paper.

   Your instructor can give you suggestions for organizing your paper and show you how to give credit to those whose ideas or actual words you are borrowing.

MAKING CONNECTIONS

The word *frontiers* originally meant a borderland; however, at least in American usage, the definition has grown much broader with time. In the nineteenth century it often referred to cheap, plentiful land, which was available to those with the strength and courage to tame it. Now the word has come to refer to any area of activity that gives the opportunity for advancement and achievement. Based on the essays in this unit (as well as others in the text that you might want to consider), what would be your extended definition of *frontier*? Can you think of other frontiers besides those in this unit or text?

ACKNOWLEDGMENTS

Jack Agueros: "Halfway to Dick and Jane," from *The Immigrant Experience* edited by Thomas Wheeler. Copyright © 1971 by the Dial Press. Reprinted by permission of Doubleday & Company, Inc.

Sherwood Anderson: "Discovery of a Father." Copyright © 1939 by the Reader's Digest Association, Inc. Copyright renewed 1966 by Eleanor Copenhaver Anderson. Reprinted by permission of Harold Ober Associates Incorporated.

Maya Angelou: "I Know Why the Caged Bird Sings," from *I Know Why the Caged Bird Sings* by Maya Angelou. Copyright © 1969 by Maya Angelou. Reprinted by permission of Random House, Inc.

Arthur Ashe: "Send Your Children to the Libraries." Copyright © 1977 by The New York Times Company. Reprinted by permission.

Pete Axthelm: "Where Have All the Heroes Gone?" Copyright 1979 by Newsweek, Inc. All rights reserved. Reprinted by permission.

John C. Bennett: "My First Hunting Trip." Reprinted by permission of John C. Bennett.

Louise Bernikow: "Never Too Old: The Art of Getting Better," from *Mademoiselle* Magazine, March 1983. Copyright © 1983 by Condé Nast Publications, Inc., and Louise Bernikow. Reprinted by permission of Louise Bernikow.

Jennifer Bitner: "Women Wasted." Reprinted by permission of Jennifer Bitner. This article is published here for the first time. Permission to reprint must be obtained from the publisher.

Frederic Brown: "The Answer." Copyright © 1954 by Frederic Brown. Reprinted by permission of Roberta Pryor, Inc.

Art Buchwald: "Sex Ed—The Pros and Cons," from *Down the Seine and Up the Potomac with Art Buchwald* by Art Buchwald. Copyright © 1971, 1972, 1973 by Art Buchwald. Reprinted by permission of G. P. Putnam's Sons.

Shirley Chisholm: "I'd Rather Be Black Than Female," from *McCall's,* August 1970. Reprinted by permission of Shirley Chisholm.

Colette Dowling: "The Cinderella Complex," Copyright © 1982 by Colette Dowling. Reprinted by permission of Summit Books, a division of Simon & Schuster, Inc.

Catherine Ettlinger: "Skiing with the Guys." Reprinted with permission from *Working Woman* Magazine. Copyright © 1987 by Working Woman/McCall's Group.

Marjorie Franco: "Yes, Women and Men Can Be 'Just Friends.'" Reprinted from *Today's Health,* May 1975, by special permission. © 1975 Family Media, Inc. All rights reserved.

Robert Frost: "House Fear," from *The Poetry of Robert Frost,* edited by Edward Connery Lathem. Copyright 1916, © 1969 by Holt, Rinehart and Winston. Copyright 1944 by Robert Frost. Reprinted by permission of Henry Holt and Company, Inc.

Don Gold: "Until the Singing Stops," from *Until the Singing Stops* by Don Gold. Copyright © 1979 by Don Gold. Reprinted by permission of Henry Holt and Company, Inc.

Steven Graves: "The First Kiss." Reprinted by permission of Steven Graves.

Ryan Hardesty: "Whisper the Past." Reprinted by permission of Ryan Hardesty.

Jennifer Harrison: "My Favorite Sister." Reprinted by permission of Jennifer Harrison.

Edwin A. Hoey: "Foul Shot," from *Read,* 1962. Reprinted by permission of Xerox Education Publications.

Langston Hughes: "Salvation," from *The Big Sea* by Langston Hughes. Copyright 1940 by Langston Hughes. Copyright renewed 1968 by Arna Bontemps and George Houston Bass. Reprinted by permission of Hill and Wang (now a division of Farrar, Straus and Giroux, Inc.).

Robert Jastrow: "Our Brain's Successor," from *Science Digest,* March 1981. Reprinted by permission of Robert Jastrow.

Garrison Keillor: "After a Fall." Copyright © 1982 by Garrison Keillor. Originally in *The New Yorker.* Excerpted from "After a Fall," first published June 21, 1982. Reprinted by permission of Ellen Levine Literary Agency, Inc.

Photos:
xviii: Owen Franken/Stock, Boston; 22 and 240: © Charles Harbutt/Archive Pictures; 52: Alan Carey/The Image Works; 72: Bruce Davidson/© 1970 Magnum Photos; 102: © Ellis Herwig/Stock, Boston; 130: Charles Gatewood/The Image Works; 162: © Eve Arnold/Magnum Photos; 188: Bob Adelman/Magnum Photos; 212: © 1985 Oliver R. Pierce/Stock, Boston.